"*Taking Flight* is an important proj... of diverse voices to discuss the issues facing women in our world today. It is refreshing and challenging to read a book like this that provides strong theological groundings, historical perspectives and examples from today's world that are both instructive and insightful. I would highly recommend this book."

Christine Sine
Executive Director Mustard Seed Associates, speaker, teacher, and author of *Tales of a Seasick Doctor, Survival of the Fittest: Keeping Healthy in Overseas Travel* and Service, and *Sacred Rhythms: Finding a Peaceful Pace in a Hectic World*

"Wow. I found *Taking Flight* to be a thoroughly captivating book from the first page. It is thoughtful and provoking, relevant but never reactionary. It is full of Scriptural precedents and historical background while offering prophetic insight as to what's coming up next. So many issues of great importance and all of them dealt with fairly and passionately."

Andrew Jones
The Boaz Project, tallskinnykiwi.com

"*Taking Flight* lives up to its title! The collaborative nature of this project gives witness to the power and creativity of a Christ-centered community rather than futile discursive matches. When grounded in Christ, it is possible to soar in hope that men and women serving together can be reconciling forces in a world desperately needing our full attention and contributions. Thoroughly enjoyed reading it!"

Dr. MaryKate Morse
author of *Making Room for Leadership* and professor at George Fox Seminary

Wikiklesia Project: Volume 2

Taking Flight: Reclaiming the Female Half of God's Image Through Advocacy and Renewal

Cynthia La Grou
Caleb J Seeling
editors

Copyright © 2010 Wikiklesia Press
Wikiklesia Press / www.wikiklesia.org
ISBN-13: 978-0-9796856-3-7

"The Words of God Do Not Justify Cruelty to Women" by President Carter used by permission—special thanks to the Carter Foundation.

Internet addresses (websites, blogs, etc.) and telephone numbers printed in this book are offered as a resource to you. These are not intended in any way to be or imply an endorsement on the part of Wikiklesia or Samizdat Creative Services, nor do we vouch for the content of these sites and numbers for the life of this book.

All rights reserved. No part of this publication may be reproduced, stored in a retrieval system, or transmitted in any form or by any means—electronic, mechanical, photocopy, recording, or any other—except for brief quotations in printed reviews, without the prior permission.

Cover design and interior art by Cynthia LaGrou
Interior design by Samizdat Creative Services

Published in association with Samizdat Creative Services
http://samizdatcreative.com

Taking Flight:

Reclaiming the Female Half of God's Image Through Advocacy and Renewal

Cynthia La Grou
Caleb J Seeling

Editors

Wikiklesia Project: Volume 2

Table of Contents

Introduction

1. What God Has Joined Together . . .
Linda Mader — 13

2. Reimagining Women's Role in the Church
Frank Viola — 29

3. Change is in the Wind: Taking Flight
Cynthia La Grou — 67

4. Women of the Kingdom
Felicity Dale — 89

5. Leadership Lenses, Jungian Archetypes, and Gender
Leonard Hjalmarson — 103

6. Kingdom of God or Men?: Questions for Thinking Through Our Cultural Context
Brad Sargent — 119

7. Why We Need Mothers & Fathers, Sisters & Brothers, Daughters & Sons
Kathy Escobar — 135

8. Coloring Outside the Christian Circle
Becky Garrison — 149

9. Women Hold the Keys to a Sustainable Future
Anna Clark — 157

10 Opportunities for Seminary-Trained Women: Past, Present, and Future
Vaun Swanson — 175

11 The Sophia Network: Activists for Change
Jenny Baker — 195

12 Shoulders to Stand On: Men's Role in Restoring the Woman's Voice
Jeff McQuilkin — 211

13 Dancing As Well As Weeping
Thomas Hohstadt — 223

14 The Weakest Foot Forward
Angie and Todd Fadel — 231

15 Fruit-Basket Turnover: From Brick to Organic Faith Communities
Jeremy Smith — 241

16 The Words of God Do Not Justify Cruelty to Women
President Jimmy Carter — 249

17 The Courageous Imagination: A Call to Men
Jonathan Brink — 257

Quotes

Appendix 1
The Challenges Facing Women and Girls are Clear

Appendix 2
Belief Systems on the Roles of Women: Theological Constructs

Wikiklesia Volume 2 Taking Flight
Introduction

Women's flight paths are shifting radically, as they intuitively harness the winds of change and rise to the challenges of the next century. The church is beginning to change dramatically as well, as people migrate toward more experiential and participatory settings which deemphasize hierarchically dominant structures. The widening opportunity to implement community rich, decentralized structures, however, cannot be fully realized without women, who are naturally inclined to flourish in these types of environments. But where will women's sights be set and where will their influence be most felt? And what might the final flight destination look like? Does it matter and if so how will it affect us all?

This book asks these questions and more: How can we transcend paralyzing controversy to work together as men and women of faith within a cultural framework that is gathering around pressing global issues, service-based action, and gender inclusion as an inherent part of its ethical and spiritual landscape? How can we turn away from our deep subconscious bias and centuries of devaluation and discrimination to move toward positive, unified action?

Introduction

Wikiklesia Volume Two is a selection of established and renegade authors, bloggers, and practitioners who come from diverse backgrounds to tackle challenging subjects that people care and talk about. The editors and authors represented here may not be in complete agreement with all the ideas and chapters in this book, and the readers are free to disagree, but I feel that they raise a few of the contextual, social, and spiritual issues that we need to face as we rethink not only how to enter the next century, but how to view and treat one another in Christ's love—thus presenting a unified image of God.

Selection of this theme was based not only on the lack of relevant published material (and the editors interest in the topic), but also on the participation throughout the blogosphere whenever the topic came up. We noticed the needs of an audience who was looking for options, yet felt there were no practical solutions outside of the discussion. We think *Taking Flight* will provide some fresh perspectives.

It is not a collection of essays about theology, gender equality, or women in leadership—although these topics are mentioned. It is an anthology focused on living in right relationship with each other in inclusive, Christ-centered communities through forms of mutual submission and blended authority, based on gifting and humility (rather than gender) which restores dignity, achieves balance, and empowers all. How that is modeled authentically in personal, professional, local, and global settings will inspire others and have a lasting impact on the human family and the planet.

Gender segregation or focusing on empowering one sex over the other has not and will not benefit anyone in the long run. It serves humanity and better fits God's original design when men and women support one another, humbly honoring their differences as integral positives rather than detriments. We need to understand how culture is changing, how to promote shared leadership, and how to employ the methods of reconciliation given in God's word.

"Easy to say, but *impossible!*" you might shout in frustration. Perhaps, but concerted effort will always pave the way for new approaches, discoveries, blessings, and benefits. The process of reconciliation is not a program, but based on relationship and it takes time to unfold. Forgiveness from the injured party is key, but the final outcome must be desired by all who are on the journey. God's mission of reconciliation in a broken world cannot be authentic unless dignity has been restored to those who've had it withheld.

—Cynthia La Grou

About Wikiklesia

The award winning Wikiklesia Project is an experiment in personal participatory media and on-line collaborative publishing. The lines between traditional and online publishing are starting to blur, and technology and delivery models are rapidly changing.

Wikiklesia has created a *between-publishing* paradigm based on collaboration over copyright. The model is flexible and nomadic. It is conversational, community building, and open source, exploring new publishing paradigms that not only create streams of information and crowd sourced narrative, but which have the potential to generate social movement and raise money for charities.

Introduction

Proceeds from Taking Flight *will go toward the formation of a women's global stewardship (leadership) database and resource center. Once established the community will direct funds into a chosen charity. Emancipation Network is first on the list—http://www.madebysurvivors.com.*

Wikiklesia Volume 2 Taking Flight
What God Has Joined Together . . .
Linda Mader

"Just then his disciples returned and were surprised to find him talking with a woman." (John 4:27)

The disciples and people of Jesus' day were not ready for the radical love and acceptance that he manifested in their midst. Within the church, there are still some who would be surprised to find Jesus talking to, or through, a woman.

The perception of women in leadership is tied to a polarized debate over gender issues. This debate is centered on a myopic perspective of a few specific scriptures interpreted through the grids of tradition and organizational structures.

Perhaps by approaching this issue from a different perspective it might be possible to break through the polarity of the debate to find a constructive narrative and context for the participation of women in the church. Doing so requires a willingness to set aside assumptions and to take a comprehensive view of the narrative of scripture.

A narrative understanding of unity

In the beginning God created man—a being created in His image, an expression that was both male and female. God took this man Adam and put him in the garden. And then God said, "This is *not* good."

As a solitary being, man did not and could not express the relational nature of God. Differentiation was needed in order to reflect the dynamic relationship that God experiences in trinitarian life. God created this differentiation by dividing man into beings that were now distinctly male and female.

In this creative act, He established the dynamics of relationship that allowed for differentiation and connection, for diversity and unity-within-diversity. The distinction between male and female was declared good and God blessed their maleness and their femaleness. He blessed their unity and their community.

When mankind was deceived, the perfection of this relational dynamic became distorted. God warned Adam and Eve that sin would impact the essence of their relationship. He explained that selfishness and control would be a part of their ongoing struggle. He cautioned that frustrated desires and the exercise of power would contaminate the unity they had known.

This became the reality of the human experience.

All social relationships—marriages, families, government, religion, and entire cultures—now manifest this brokenness of relationship. Rarely do we witness the true beauty of unity and diversity that was originally intended.

Instead, relationships are marred with twisted perceptions of authority and power. The distortion is so pervasive, that some are convinced that structures of hierarchy are God's intended purpose in marriage and the church. Imitating the world's structures of positional power, they claim that this is God's way.

A new Adam

> *"Since the children have flesh and blood, he too shared in their humanity ... For this reason he had to be made like his brothers in every way."* (Hebrews 2:14,17)

God had a plan to rescue us from our brokenness: Jesus stepped into our reality. His life manifested an entirely different way of living and being. In his humanity, Jesus experienced the temptation of competition and control. He experienced the abuse of systems of power and exclusion. He modeled a life that resisted striving and that subverted oppression by the power of love.

Jesus' life exemplified unconditional inclusion, willing submission, humble service, and self-sacrificial love. His life demonstrated the way of the kingdom, not only with miraculous signs, but also with radical inclusion of those at the margins of society.

The mystery of God's will revealed

God's plan for unity—the mystery of His will—is the adoption of His children. As members of God's household, mankind is once again united in Christ. While humanity experienced the results of sin through the disobedience of the first Adam, , His children experience the restoration of unity through the obedience of the Second Adam.

> *"He predestined us to be adopted as his sons through Jesus Christ, in accordance with his pleasure and will . . . And he made known to us the mystery of his will according to his good pleasure, which he purposed in Christ, to be put into effect when the times will have reached their fulfillment— to bring all things in heaven and on earth together under one head, even Christ."* (Ephesians 1:5,9-10)

The members of Christ's body are *one new man* reconciled through the cross. Reconciliation put division, hostility, and distinction to death.

> *"His purpose was to create in himself one new man out of the two, thus making peace, and in this one body to reconcile both of them to God through the cross, by which he put to death their hostility...Consequently, you are no longer foreigners and aliens, but fellow citizens with God's people and members of God's household."* (Ephesians 2:15-16,19)

This particular passage deals with Jews and Gentiles. However, we see in many other verses that the reconciliation accomplished at the cross destroys all former dividing lines and creates a new reality of unity in Christ.

> "... you have taken off your old self with its practices and have put on the new self, which is being renewed in knowledge in the image of its Creator. Here there is no Greek or Jew, circumcised or uncircumcised, barbarian, Scythian, slave or free, but Christ is all, and is in all ... And over all these virtues put on love, which binds them all together in perfect unity." (Colossians 3:9-11,14)

> "For we were all baptized by one Spirit into one body—whether Jews or Greeks, slave or free." (1 Corinthians 12:13)

> "You are all sons of God through faith in Christ Jesus ... There is neither Jew nor Greek, slave nor free, male nor female, for you are all one in Christ Jesus." (Galatians 3:26,28)

In Christ, man is once again united in a single Body—it's a return to the unity and connection that God intended for us from the beginning.

> "Make every effort to keep the unity of the Spirit ... There is one body and one Spirit ... one God and Father of all, who is over all and through all and in all." (Ephesians 4:3-4,6)

What God Has Joined Together . . . Linda Mader

> *". . . for we are members of his body . . . This is a profound mystery—but I am talking about Christ and the church."* (Ephesians 5:30,32)

A new creation

As a new humanity in Christ, we are to be image bearers of the divine nature.

> *"And just as we have borne the likeness of the earthly man, so shall we bear the likeness of the man from heaven."* (1 Corinthians 15:49)

> *"For those God foreknew he also predestined to be conformed to the likeness of his Son, that he might be the firstborn among many brothers."* (Romans 7:29)

The church is literally the family of God. The relationship to one another is that of brothers and sisters, children of the Father.

> *"How great is the love the Father has lavished on us, that we should be called children of God! And that is what we are."* (1 John 3:1)

> *"Both the one who makes men holy and those who are made holy are of the same family. So Jesus is not ashamed to call them brothers."* (Hebrews 2:11)

The Body of Christ is One Body. Within it, all distinctions—religious, cultural, economic, racial, and gender—no longer exist. There is equality in Christ among those who would not be considered equal according to the standards of the world. Former religious distinctions and traditions hold no relevance in regard to one's standing in Christ.

> "... so in Christ we who are many form one body, and each member belongs to all the others." (Romans 12:5)

> "God has combined the members of the body and has given greater honor to the parts that lacked it so that there should be no division in the body, but that its parts should have equal concern for each other." (1 Corinthians 12:24-25)

> "So from now on we regard no one from a worldly point of view ... if anyone is in Christ, he is a new creation." (2 Corinthians 5:16-17)

> "... you know that he who is both their Master and yours is in heaven, and there is no favoritism with him." (Ephesians 6:9)

A new way of being

Membership in God's family as His children is a spiritual reality. We are new creatures, participants in the kingdom of God.

> "... children born not of natural descent ... but born of God." (John 1:13)

What God Has Joined Together . . .   Linda Mader

Children of God live life by the Spirit, expressing a new way of being. Christ is our example of how to live this new life.

> *"Your attitude should be the same as that of Christ Jesus: Who, being in very nature God, did not consider equality with God something to be grasped, but made himself nothing, taking the very nature of a servant, being made in human likeness." (Philemon 2:5-7)*

> *"Now that I, your Lord and Teacher, have washed your feet, you also should wash one another's feet. I have set you an example that you should do as I have done for you."* (John 13:14-15)

Unity in Christ is expressed in a humble attitude toward others. At the core of relationship in community is one's perception of one's relationship to God and to others.

> *". . . but in humility consider others better than yourselves. Each of you should look not only to your own interests, but also to the interests of others."* (Philemon 2:3-4)

> *"Be devoted to one another in brotherly love. Honor one another above yourselves."* (Romans 12:10)

Jesus could not have been more clear in describing the essence of relationships among believers.

> *"Jesus said to them, "The kings of the Gentiles lord it over them; and those who exercise authority call themselves Benefactors. But you are not to be like that. Instead, the greatest among you should be like the youngest, and the one who rules like the one who serves. For who is greater, the one who is at the table or the one who serves? Is it not the one who is at the table? But* over them *I am among you as one who serves."* (Luke 22:25-27)

A new vision

The narrative of unity that runs through the New Testament describes a plan for the restoration of all that was lost. This redemptive theme is a solid foundation for the participation of women in the church, reclaiming a unified image for the Body of Christ.

To see a transformed ecclesia, the investment in current traditions and structures must be challenged, holding up unity as the essential requirement. The world is desperately waiting for the church to demonstrate the reality of the kingdom of God and the beauty of our invitation to know the love and fellowship of God.

Bound to tradition

> *"They worship me in vain; their teachings are but rules taught by men. You have let go of the commands of God and are holding on to the traditions of men. You have a fine way of setting aside the commands of God in order to observe your own traditions! ... Thus you nullify the word of God by your tradition that you have handed down. And you do many things like that."* (Mark 7:7-9,13)

Propositional approaches to Scripture, and doctrine based upon proof texts divorced from the wider context of God's story, are inadequate for the theology of the future. There will be conflict wherever the narrative of unity challenges traditional doctrine. Those who are heavily invested in existing traditions and structures will fight against unity.

Doctrines that divide or exclude are "mere natural instincts" and do not have the Spirit. To resist serving one another in love is to indulge the sinful nature. Making distinctions that Jesus does not make is putting man-made yokes on the necks of others and hindering the kingdom.

> *"The greatest among you will be your servant. For whoever exalts himself will be humbled, and whoever humbles himself will be exalted. "Woe to you, teachers of the law and Pharisees, you hypocrites! You shut the kingdom of heaven in men's faces. You yourselves do not enter, nor will you let those enter who are trying to."* (Matthew 23:11-13)

"Who will rule?" is an invalid question in regard to leadership within the church, regardless of gender. Jesus' intent was the kingdom of God, and when He said not to rule over one another, He really meant it. Jesus had harsh words for those who elevated themselves, "who have the most important seats and the places of honor."

The people of God are to be one flesh and to have relationships of union, not hierarchy. To rule over a brother or sister is to be in a position that God never intended. This is ultimately damaging to both persons.

Defining relationship through the lens of mutuality would make a huge impact in transforming the life of the church body. Mutuality provides the freedom to love and submit to one another in authentic relationship. Hierarchy imposes a power structure on relationships and distorts the beauty God intended. When power and control remove freedom by demanding submission, requirement subverts relationship.

What one believes about the dynamics of power and equality in the kingdom is made manifest in relationships. The church must be willing to embody mutual submission, and to address structural systems and the use of power within those structures. This may necessitate a radical shift in ecclesiology.

The kingdom reality

Rediscovering a theology of the kingdom of God is vital to understanding the ecclesia. By not comprehending the kingdom and how the church fits in God's story, the church has not rightly understood its own nature. The gospel of Jesus is the gospel of the kingdom of God. The church cannot move forward without orienting itself to this reality.

The present reality of the kingdom of God has not been the guiding truth, but instead the church has been shaped by organizations and denominations. Discussions of ecclesiology must be centered on the kingdom of God rather than on structures, models, and methods.

The church must represent the reality of the kingdom in the area of equality, where there is no longer exclusion for females. Sadly, today it is the place most likely to exclude women. Looking at the standard of the kingdom of God, there is no support for this exclusion.

The body of Christ is to become a representative model of inclusion and participation that embraces the voice of the marginalized, whoever that might be, including women. It is to be the redemptive society that exemplifies equality and the inclusion of everyone, whether they are considered the greatest or the least in society.

This is the kingdom prepared since the creation of the world. While some truths were hidden since the fall, the kingdom restores the reality of oneness that once was intended for man. In this realm—the last and the least, the tax collectors and the prostitutes, the insignificant and the small—are included and valued. Scripture warns that if the church will not express this reality, *"the kingdom of God will be taken away from you and given to a people who will produce its fruit."* (Matthew 21:43)

The pattern of the world is to use hierarchical power structures, but it is not supposed to be that way among disciples. The kingdom is to be a radical overthrowing of hierarchy. Relationships with one another are to be relationships of mutual submission, serving, and preferring one another. This underlying message seems obvious and pervasive throughout the New Testament.

The beauty of *perichoresis*

"... I am in my Father, and you are in me, and I am in you."
(John 14:20)

The nature of the Trinity and the invitation to join in their relationship is also fundamental to the identity of the people of God. The Father, Son, and Holy Spirit are the example of unity in relationships. They model perfect mutual submission and deference to one another.

The Spirit is beckoning the church to become an accurate reflection of Trinitarian relationship. The church is challenged to reflect the indwelling, *perichoretic* nature of the Trinity—unity, love, interdependence, creativity, intimacy, devotion—by becoming communities of profound inclusion, love, and service.

Regardless of the fact that this may be outside the realm of religious tradition and established models of church, it is to be the pattern of relationship for believers with God and with one another. This life of unity among believers is to be a witness to the world of God's intention to creating the world for inclusion in His life and love.

This is beautifully expressed in the Jesus' prayer. Let his prayer stir in your heart a vision for restoration of the unity He desires.

> *"... [May] all of them may be one, Father, just as you are in me and I am in you. May they also be in us so that the world may believe that you have sent me. I have given them the glory that you gave me, that they may be one as we are one: I in them and you in me. May they be brought to complete unity to let the world know that you sent me and have loved them even as you have loved me."* (John 17:21-22)

We have seen in this essay that Scripture shows us the big picture of unity that God intended from before the creation of the world—that the mystery of His will is for His family to become one flesh in Christ. To continue in traditions that divide is to shatter the unity and mutual interconnectedness that He desires among His children.

Beautiful, radical, perichoretic, one-flesh unity is to be the pattern for relationships among believers.

> *"So they are no longer two, but one. Therefore what God has joined together, let man not separate."* (Matthew 19:6)

Linda is a wife, mother, friend, and Christ-follower in South Dakota. She works alongside her husband in their business and is currently working on a master's degree in leadership.

Wikiklesia Volume 2 Taking Flight
Reimagining Women's Role in the Church
Frank Viola

Subjugation of women, in fact, is a symptom of man's fallen nature. If the work of Christ involves the breaking of the entail [inherited consequences] of the fall, the implication of his work for the liberation of women is plain. Unwarranted assumptions have sometimes been drawn from the fact that all twelve of the original apostles were men. But in fact our Lord's male disciples cut a sorry figure alongside his female disciples . . . He treated women in a completely natural and unselfconscious way as real persons. He imparted his teaching to the eager ears and heart of Mary of Bethany, while to the Samaritan woman (of all people) he revealed the nature of true worship. His disciples who found him thus engaged at the well were surprised to find him talking to a woman: for a religious teacher to do this was at best a waste of time and at worst a spiritual danger.
-F.F. Bruce

"In the last days, God says, I will pour out my Spirit on all people. Your sons and daughters will prophesy, your young men will see visions, your old men will dream dreams. Even on my servants, both men and women, I will pour out my Spirit in those days, and they will prophesy."
-Peter quoting the prophet Joel in Acts 2:17-18, NIV

Dear sister,

Thank you for your gracious letter. You've asked an excellent question: What is my view on a woman's role in the church and how do I understand the "limiting passages" that seem to restrict their ministry?

To be honest, I'm monumentally disinterested in adding more noise to the ill-fated gender brawl that rages in some Christian circles. It is for this reason that I've been loathe to write on the subject. Yet I keep meeting women who have been spiritually straight-jacketed by what I find to be a wooden interpretation of certain Biblical texts. Their stories have provoked me to tread on this hazardous minefield. And for their sake, as well as for the sake of all my beloved sisters in Christ, I regret not having done so sooner.

With that said, I'm now ready to have my ears singed with the hand-wringing, nitpicking, nail-biting, and tooth-gnashing that may be generated by my response.

So let this letter forever settle the whole controversy. Here, dear sister, is the answer to your question, the final word on the subject:

Paul put it plainly when he said that under no condition and under no circumstance may a woman speak in a church meeting. She must never, ever, under any situation, say a word in the church. She must without exception keep absolutely, totally, and completely silent.

Unless . . . she has her head covered!

Are you clear now?

I trust you are laughing, for I was being facetious. Yet I was also trying to make a point. The fact is that Paul seems to contradict himself on this subject. The so-called "limiting passages" are incredibly difficult to interpret. Given their obscurity, no one can be dogmatic as to what Paul really meant when he penned them. This being so, every interpretation that's been given to these texts has shortcomings. And I will shamelessly admit that this applies to my own.

For the sake of those reading this letter over my shoulder, the "limiting passages" are those texts that seem to put some restriction on a woman's ministry in the church. Interestingly, there are only two such passages in all the New Testament. Here they are:

> *"Let the women keep silent in the churches; for they are not permitted to speak, but let them subject themselves, just as the Law also says. And if they desire to learn anything, let them ask their own husbands at home; for it is improper for a woman to speak in the church."* (1 Corinthians 14:34-35, NASB)

> *"Let a woman learn in silence with full submission. I permit no woman to teach or to have authority over a man; she is to keep silent. For Adam was formed first, then Eve; and Adam was not deceived, but the woman was deceived and become a transgressor."* (1 Timothy 2:11-14, NRSV)

Before we discuss these two passages, let me explain how I arrived at my conclusions.

The entire thrust of the New Covenant

Long ago I learned an invaluable lesson: The New Testament should never be handled as a manual of floatable doctrines and isolated teachings. The New Testament is a whole. It's essentially a story. What is written in the letters of Paul and others is part of that story.

The New Testament story contains a consistent message. It's the message of the New Covenant. This covenant is not an updating of the Old Covenant. It doesn't include a new set of rules to replace the old set of rules.

The Old Covenant contained a set of rules by which men and women were to live. It also drew sharp distinctions between people, granting special privileges to certain ones. Some were worthy to be God's people (Jews). Others were not (Gentiles). Among those who were worthy, some were given the honor of being nearest to God (the priests). Others were not (the people). Some were given special ministerial functions (the sons of Aaron). Others were given less important functions (the Levites). Still others were given virtually no function at all (the congregation).

When Jesus Christ entered the scene, all of this radically changed. Our Lord inaugurated a New Covenant which made the old one obsolete. The New Covenant did away with rules. It did away with earthly distinctions. And it abolished special classes of people who possessed special privileges.

Under the New Covenant, the Law of God has been written on the human heart by the Holy Spirit. The Spirit has come to indwell all who call upon the Savior—including men and women. Including Jew and Gentile. Including slaves and non-slaves.

All earthly distinctions have been abolished by the New Covenant. All ministerial classes have been wiped out. To possess the Spirit means to have access to God—no one excluded.

In addition, possessing the Spirit means being granted the privilege to minister in God's house. As Peter quotes the prophet Joel:

> *"In the last days, God says, I will pour out my Spirit on all people. Your sons and daughters will prophesy, your young men will see visions, your old men will dream dreams. Even on my servants, both men and women, I will pour out my Spirit in those days, and they will prophesy."* (Joel 2:28-29; Acts 2:17-18, NIV)

Galatians 3:28 sums up the New Covenant nicely: *"There is neither Jew nor Greek, bond nor free, male nor female, for you are all one in Christ Jesus."* This passage summarizes Paul's understanding of the effect of the gospel on cultural givens like racism, slavery, and gender oppression. Galatians 3:28 is not constricted to "salvation." Instead, it holds social implications for everyone.

In short, the New Covenant erases all social and class distinctions. And it has afforded all to receive the Spirit and serve as priests in God's house. That includes women. With that said, whatever the "limiting passages" mean, they cannot in any way overturn the New Covenant. Neither can they contradict the entire thrust of the New Testament. Hence, the idea that women are excluded from speaking in God's house is a catastrophic breach of the New Covenant—a Covenant that has done away with earthly distinctions and treats both men and women as co-priests in God's kingdom.

The invisible interpreter

Another lesson I learned in my spiritual journey has to do with the reality of the Holy Spirit. I'm a firm believer in the intuitive work of the Holy Spirit in the life of the believer. I also hold squarely to the organic nature of the Body of Christ.

The indwelling Spirit gives every believer Divine instincts and impulses that are just as real as our physical senses. Because the Spirit and the Scripture are born out of Divine inspiration, the leading of the Spirit will never contradict Scripture. Nor will the Scripture contradict the instincts of the Spirit.

With that said, on a purely subjective level, all my spiritual instincts tell me that God wants women to function in the meetings of the church. I have observed house church meetings and small group fellowships where the women were muzzled. They were prohibited from uttering a word. Only the men spoke. As I sat in those gatherings, everything inside me intuitively knew that this was amiss. There was something shamefully artificial about it all, especially when there were women in the same room who were richer in spiritual life than many of the men. But they were vetoed from speaking simply because they were women.

This practice, to my mind, violates an important spiritual principle. Everything in the Lord's house is governed by *"the measure of Christ"* (Ephesians 4:13). Yet these meetings were governed by external restrictions which produced spiritual limitation. When women who have a great spiritual contribution to make are restricted from speaking in the gatherings of the church, the Body suffers for it.

I'll articulate the clear impressions I had in those meetings as I watched the men wax eloquent (or ramble on) while the sisters passively spectated: Half the priesthood of God is being smothered and squelched. The sisters are banned from speaking simply because the brothers have intellectually interpreted the Bible to mean that they should be quiet. It seems they are blithely ignoring what their spiritual instincts are telling them about the practical fruit of this interpretation. This meeting is grossly lacking in spiritual richness. It reminds me of the so-called "real world" in the movie *The Matrix*—cold, colorless, and tasteless. Muting the sisters is a good recipe for producing highly academic, sterile meetings.

When I stepped back from that experience of watching the sisters sit in their seats dumbly, I had to ask myself a telling question: What clear message is sent by silencing the sisters in the church meetings? The answer is as arresting as it is alarming. The undeniable message is that men cannot learn anything from women. Nor can they be ministered to spiritually by a woman.

Please ponder that for a moment.

If every brother were honest with himself, he would be forced to admit that such a thought is absurd. It's also a poor fit with real life. My observation is that those who hold to the idea that women must be silent in the church "because the Bible says so" are doing something that's quite plastic. I mean, what man in his right mind (provided that his IQ is higher than that of a carrot) really believes that he can't learn spiritual things from a woman? Such a belief strains the bounds of credulity until they break.

In my own experience, some of the most flooring insights shared in church meetings have come from the lips of women. Their contributions have been profoundly rich and meaningful. The women also bring an element in their sharing that men do not. It's the fragrance of Jesus Christ. Interestingly, throughout Scripture, when the aroma of the Lord is mentioned, women are always involved (Psalm 45:7-9; Luke 23:55-24:1; John 12:3). Women have a unique way of emitting the fragrance of Christ's life to others.

I shall argue, therefore, that the practice of silencing woman in a meeting is something outwardly imposed rather than the natural expression of authentic Body life.

What would happen if . . . ?

Imagine for a moment that the two "limiting texts" didn't appear in the New Testament. What would be the practice of those churches that don't allow their women to speak in the meetings? What would the women prefer to do? Such an acute question—if it can be answered—is profoundly insightful. If the church would allow the sisters to speak in their gatherings, then one must question if the practice of silencing them contradicts the natural life of the Spirit. To my mind, it does.

Interestingly, some of the men who hold to the "women-must-be-silent" doctrine have admitted to me that they are puzzled as to why God asks for such a thing. Some of them have highly lauded the contributions of their wives in spiritual matters . . . only to express confusion as to why they can't share such contributions in public gatherings. I applaud these men's desire to be faithful to their understanding of Scripture. But I challenge the accuracy of that understanding on both spiritual and Biblical grounds. And I would urge them to re-examine their interpretation based on these deeper observations.

Parenthetically, I'm keenly aware that there do exist men who are chauvinistic, gender-hierarchical, patriarchical, sexist (pick-your-adjective) legalists who have been oppressing females all their lives. These befuddled souls are eager to latch onto any Bible verse that can be twisted to billy-club women. They are quite clever at masking their own personal biases against women with Scripture verses. And they will judge anyone who defends women speaking in the church as pursuing a modernist heresy. But I'm not appealing to such people in this letter. They probably couldn't get past the first page.

On the flip side, I've been in scores of meetings where the women spoke with the men present. All of the churches I work with do so. The immense spiritual benefit to both the sisters and the brothers during such meetings is undeniable. In addition, the spirit of every believer in the room knows that it's both proper and necessary for women to function and share Christ. And the marks of the Holy Spirit's presence—"life and peace"—are unquestionably present (Romans 8:6).

In this connection, in every organic expression of the church that I'm aware of, the sisters function in the meetings as do the brothers. (This has been true in my own experience ever since I began meeting in homes in the late 1980s.) To my mind, it's only when we get exposed to the "limiting passages" and adopt a certain interpretation of them that things begin to change. When this happens, some Christians devolve from liberty to suppression. This is never a sign of God's fingerprints, for *"where the Spirit of the Lord is, there is liberty"* (2 Corinthians 3:17).

Now before someone reading this letter clips the previous paragraphs out of context and labels me a "spiritual subjectivist" . . . and before I'm accused of exalting my own subjective leadings above the Scriptures (which I predict someone will do) . . . let me repeat what I said at the front. The Scripture and the internal witness of the Spirit always go hand-in-hand. Consequently, if our interpretation of the Bible smacks square in the face of what our human spirit is telling us . . . and if it flat-footedly denies what is practically real in our own lives (that men can learn spiritual things from women), this should force us to seriously re-examine our interpretation of certain Biblical passages.

I said all that to make a simple point: My interpretation of the "limiting passages" perfectly mirrors what my spirit tells me is right, proper, natural, and spiritually viable in a church meeting. It also maps perfectly to those organic expressions of the church with which I'm familiar. Thus on a spiritual, practical, and intellectual plane, I'm at peace with it.

I suggest that anyone who wishes to upgrade their thinking on this subject take all three elements (spiritual, practical, and intellectual) into consideration. Disregarding one can easily lead to a skewed perspective. To put it another way, the culture of organic church life precludes any interpretation of the "limiting passages" that bans women from speaking in church meetings.

What saith the big picture?

A basic question must be answered at this point: What is the overall teaching of the New Testament on a woman's role in the church? That is, what's the big picture about women in ministry? You'll find that it's perfectly consistent with the broad principles of the New Covenant. What follows, therefore, is a chronological survey of women in ministry in the New Testament. Since I don't have a concordance in front of me, I'm doing this from less than inspired memory:

> Elizabeth and Mary (not Zachariah and Joseph) are the first to receive the message of Christ's birth into the world. They are honored and blessed by angels. They are also the first to sing and prophesy about the Christ child. The prophetess Anna receives honorable mention as one who speaks of the Messiah to those who have waited for Him (Luke 2:36-38).

> During our Lord's earthly ministry, a group that Luke calls the Women were just as well known as the Twelve (Luke 8:1-3; 23:49, 55; 24:24). In fact, the twelve male disciples were a rather pitiful bunch when compared to the Lord's female disciples (see Luke 16).

> Both the Twelve and the Women were among the 120 who waited for the coming of the Holy Spirit on the day of Pentecost (Acts 1:14). The Women, along with the men, spoke in tongues, declaring the "great things of God" (Acts 2:1-11).

> The Holy Spirit was poured out upon women and men alike—the result being that "your daughters shall prophesy" (Acts 2:17-18).

In Christ, all earthly barriers have been destroyed. Galatians 3:28 boldly declares, "There is neither Jew nor Greek, there is neither bond nor free, there is neither male nor female: for ye are all one in Christ Jesus." Women, therefore, are not second-class citizens in the church of God.

Paul and Silas plant a church in Philippi. It begins with all women. Lydia is one of them. She hosts the church meetings in her home. So, it's inconceivable to think that the women in the church in Philippi could not speak or function in the meetings. (Acts 16:12ff.).

Priscilla and her husband, Aquila, teach Apollos the way of the Lord more fully (Acts 18:26). It's noteworthy that four out of the six times that Priscilla and Aquila are mentioned in the New Testament, Priscilla's name appears first (Acts 18:18, 26; Rom. 16:3; 2 Tim. 4:19). This is ancient shorthand signifying that Priscilla was more spiritually prominent. Also, the fact that her name appears first when she and her husband instructed Apollos indicates that she led in that exchange (Acts 18:26, NASB and NIV).

Philip the evangelist had four daughters who were prophetesses (Acts 21:9). This means they prophesied. Note that first-century prophecy was always done in and among the church. Question: If a woman is prophesying by God's Spirit, why on earth would a man be barred from hearing it?

In 1 Corinthians 11:4-5, Paul says that women may both pray and prophesy when the church comes together (1 Corinthians 11:1-34). The context of this passage makes clear that Paul is referring to public meetings where both men and women are present (1 Corinthians 11-14).

When Paul wrote his letter to the Roman Christians, he honored the following women for their service in the church: Phoebe, Priscilla, Mary, Tryphena, Tryphosa, Persis, Julia, and the sister of Nereus (Romans 16). Paul lists about twice as many men as women. But he commends more than twice as many women as he does men.

In Romans 16:2, Paul calls Phoebe a *prostatis*, which means "one who stands in front of, superintends, guards, and provides care for others." The word is a derivative of *proistemi*, which is used in Romans 12:8, 1 Thessalonians 5:12, and 1 Timothy 5:17.

Paul mentions Junia as a fellow-apostle (Romans 16:7). This is the most natural way to construe the statement "notable among the apostles." And "Junia" is clearly a feminine name.[1]

In Philippians 4:2-3, Paul makes special mention of Euodias and Syntyche who helped him in the Lord's work.

Paul reminds Titus that the older women should be "teachers of good things." They should also to teach the younger women (Titus 2:3-5).

Paul commends Timothy's mother and grandmother. We can reasonably infer that these two women taught Timothy the Holy Scriptures since he was a child (2 Timothy 1:5; 3:15).

---

[1] See Eldon Jay Epp's *Junia: The First Woman Apostle* (Minneapolis: Fortress, 2005).

Clearly, women were active in ministry in the first-century church. Because they were recipients of the Holy Spirit, they were just as much a part of the believing priesthood as were the men. We find them prophesying publicly. Praying publicly. Teaching publicly. We also find them "contending side by side" with Paul in God's work. In addition, Paul calls some women "co-workers," a term he uses for his male associates.

That said, some have interpreted the "limiting passages" to mean that women must *de facto* be excluded from sharing in a meeting when men are present. But this conclusion runs against the grain of the broad principles of the New Testament. For this reason, advocates of the "women-must-not-speak" position are forced into completely non-Scriptural dances to distinguish "sharing" (when only sisters are present) and "teaching" (when men are present). But this is pure invention. And it's dissonant with the Biblical context. There's no evidence anywhere that Paul or his entourage ever excluded anyone from ministry on the basis of gender. Paul happily worked alongside women like Priscilla, Euodias, and Syntyche without any supercilious hokum about Divinely-ordained female inferiority. Further, there's no analog for the "women-cannot-speak-with-men-present" idea in any of Paul's other letters. In short, both of Paul's letters are consistent with the revolutionary sentiment that he voiced in Galatians 3The truth of the matter is that the "limiting passages" are highly obscure. Anyone who asserts that they are clear and direct is living in a fog of presumption and academic naivety. For one thing, such an assertion reflects a benighted dismissal of texts like Acts 2:17, Galatians 3:28, and 1 Corinthians 11:5, 14:26, 31.

Pick up any decent commentary. Look up the "limiting passages," and you'll discover the various ways these texts can be interpreted due to the ambiguity of the language. The fact that competent evangelical scholars disagree on the leaning of Paul's word usage in these passages attests to their obscurity. It's my opinion that we should always interpret the obscure by the clear, not the other way around. When we interpret the clear and consistent thrust of Scripture in light of one or two obscure passages, we end up rupturing the core message of the Bible. And we are forced to do all sorts of exegetical gymnastics to make the many clear passages fit our interpretation of the few obscure texts.

Therefore, when an obscure passage seems to be at odds with the clear thrust of Scripture, we must look carefully at context.

What kind of "silence" is this?

Attention to context—historical, social, local, and spiritual—is crucial when it comes to rightly interpreting a passage of Scripture. So let's look at the local context of the first "limiting passage" in 1 Corinthians 14:29-35:

> *"Let two or three prophets speak, and let the others pass judgment. But if a revelation is made to another who is seated, let the first one keep silent. For you can all prophesy one by one, so that all may learn and all may be exhorted; and the spirits of prophets are subject to prophets; for God is not a God of confusion but of peace, as in all the churches. Let the women keep silent in the churches; for they are not permitted to speak, but let them subject themselves, just as the Law also says. And if they desire to learn anything, let them ask their own husbands at home; for it is improper for a woman to speak in the church."* (NASB)

There are several things to consider here. First, Paul has already encouraged the women to pray and prophesy earlier in the letter (1 Corinthians 11:5). Second, Paul encourages the whole church to function in Chapter 14. He writes, *"for you can all prophesy one by one"* (v. 31) and *"when you assemble, every one of you has a psalm, has a teaching, has a revelation . . ."* (v. 26). (To assert that these exhortations don't include women is ludicrous. It's to suggest that the church doesn't include women, and the New Testament is only written to men. There is nothing in the flow of 1 Corinthians 14 that would suggest that Paul is addressing men only. In addition, Paul makes clear that the gift of prophecy—which women possess—is mainly to be exercised in the church meetings, as in 1 Corinthians 11:5; 14:4-5, 29, 31, 39.)

Therefore, for Paul to suddenly say that women must never say a word in the church meeting is to completely contradict himself in the space of a few sentences. New Testament scholars have put forth two scenarios that easily resolve the apparent discrepancy. Let's examine each one.

Scenario 1

The meetings in Corinth were in utter chaos. Many of the members were speaking in tongues at the same time, and no one was interpreting what was being spoken. Some were prophesying jointly. And what some of the prophets were saying was in dire need of evaluation. But few people were doing this.

Some in the church were doubting the resurrection (1 Corinthians 15). Others were under the impression that visiting prostitutes and committing incest were acceptable. To their minds, since these things were done with the body and not the spirit, they were innocent activities (1 Corinthians 5-6).

In the face of all this, the women were interrupting those prophesying with questions. Their motivation was to learn. But they were adding a further distraction to an already disruptive meeting.

It was common in the ancient world for hearers to interrupt someone who was teaching with questions. But it was considered rude if the questions reflected ignorance of the subject.

It must be noted that women in the first century—whether Jew or Gentile—tended to be uneducated. Any exception was rare. Women were essentially trained to be home-keepers. Thus for a woman to query or challenge a man in public was an embarrassing thing in the Greco-Roman world. When women interrupted the men with questions, the men were being interrogated by their social inferiors. Hence, it was considered "improper."

In 1 Corinthians 14, Paul deals with this entire mess. First, he handles the abuse and misuse of tongues and prescribes guidelines for their proper use (1 Corinthians 14:1-28). He then switches to the subject of giving and evaluating prophetic words (1 Corinthians 14:29-34). So beginning with chapter 14:29, Paul shifts his attention to the prophets and their role in the church. He tells the Corinthians that when someone prophesies, they shouldn't do so at the same time that someone else is speaking. Instead, those who prophesy should do so in turn.

It's within this very context that Paul shifts to the sisters and says that if they don't understand a prophetic word, they should ask their husbands about it in private. Their tutoring is to occur at home, not in the meeting. The meeting is not a question-answer session.

Look at the passage again with this thought in mind:

"And if they desire to learn anything, let them ask their own husbands at home; for it is improper for a woman to speak in the church."

Notice the undeniable connection between "learning" and "speaking." Therefore, the only kind of speaking that Paul is restricting in this passage is that of asking questions—both leading-questions and ignorance-based questions. It's also quite possible that the sisters were quizzing their own husbands, evaluating their prophetic words personally and pointedly. Paul doesn't want there to be any domestic disputes in the meetings, so he asks the women to question their husbands at home.

Either way, Paul's injunction for women to "keep silent" doesn't possess an absolute sense. It's a corrective to a specific problem. The context bears this out. Instead of publicly clamoring for explanations, the women were to learn from their husbands at home. However, when it came to speaking in the meeting to edify the church, they were free to speak (1 Corinthians 11:5; 14:26, 31).

To strengthen the case, the Greek word "silent" in this verse is *sigao*. It means to hold one's peace temporarily. The word has the flavor of being quiet in order to listen to what another has to say. Paul uses the same word two other times in chapter 14. He first says that the person speaking in tongues should be silent (*sigao*) if there is no interpreter

(v. 28). Does this mean that the one who speaks in tongues is never to speak in the meeting? Certainly not.

Paul uses the same word again when he says that if a person interrupts someone prophesying, the first one speaking should be silent (*sigao*), letting the other person interject his word (v. 30). Does this mean that the person prophesying should never speak again in the meeting after he has been interrupted? Certainly not.

In the same way, when a sister has a question during the church meeting, she ought to be silent (*sigao*). That is, she should hold her peace and yield the floor to the person who is speaking (v. 29-34). Does this mean that the sisters are never to speak in the meeting? Certainly not. Such a thing reflects a culturally-biased misreading of Paul. It also puts Paul in stark contradiction with himself (11:5; 14:26, 31).

No, the "silence" here has a very restricted meaning. It applies to those times when a sister was confused by something spoken or when she overtly challenged a prophetic word. Paul was saying that in such cases, the sister should hold her peace and give way to the one speaking. She should then quiz her husband at home. For Paul, this would foster both order and peace to a chaotic and confused meeting in Corinth (v. 33).

While I'm no fan of Bible paraphrases, I think Eugene Peterson's translation reflects this scenario the best:

> *"Wives must not disrupt worship, talking when they should be listening, asking questions that could more appropriately be asked of their husbands at home ... Wives have no license*

to use the time of worship for unwarranted speaking." (1 Corinthians 14:34-35, *The Message*)

Scenario 2

Some scholars have put forth a different interpretation of this text. Yet it leads to the same conclusion as the interpretation just described. In verse 34, Paul says, *"but let them [the women] subject themselves just as the law also says."* Interestingly, there is no law in the Old Testament that calls women to silence or to subject themselves. The Old Testament seems to say the opposite. For example, Psalm 68:11 says, *"The Lord gives the command; the women who proclaim the good tidings are a great host."*

What law could Paul be referring to here? Tellingly, the silencing of women was a Jewish ordinance in the ancient world. It came from the Talmud, which was the Jewish oral law during the time that Paul penned 1 Corinthians. According to the Talmud, women were not permitted to speak in the Jewish assembly or even ask questions. Consider the follow quotes from the Talmud:

> *A woman's voice is prohibited because it is sexually provocative.* (Talmud, Berachot 24a)

> *Women are sexually seductive, mentally inferior, socially embarrassing, and spiritually separated from the law of Moses; therefore, let them be silent.* (Summary of Talmudic sayings)

> *It is a shame for a woman to let her voice be heard among men.* (Talmud, Tractate Kiddushin)

The voice of a woman is filthy nakedness. (Talmud, Berachot Kiddushin)

In light of the above statements, the negative words about women in 1 Corinthians 34-35 may not have been Paul's words at all. Instead, he may have been quoting those in the Corinthian church who based their view of women on the Talmud. The Talmud taught that women couldn't speak in the assembly and added that their voices were obscene and shameful, the very thoughts that we read in verses 35 and 36.

This is further confirmed in verse 36 where Paul exclaims, *"What! Did the Word of God originate with you?"* The *"What!"* indicates that Paul wasn't in harmony with the quotation in verses 34 and 35.

We know that various concerns and questions came to Paul from the Corinthians (1:11; 7:1, 25; 8:1; 12:1). Throughout 1 Corinthians, Paul quotes some of the people in the church and then responds to their arguments (6:12, 13; 7:1; 10:23). If quotation marks are placed at the beginning and ending of verses 34 and 35, then the apparent contradiction between Paul's encouragement of female participation and his apparent silencing of them is resolved. Let's read the text with this scenario in mind. Here's the stance of some of the Corinthians, as Paul quotes it:

> *"Let the women keep silence in the churches; for they are not permitted to speak, but let them subject themselves just as the law also says. And if they desire to learn anything, let them ask their own husbands at home; for it is shameful and*

lewd for a woman to speak in church." (1 Corinthians 14:34-35)

Here's Paul's rebuttal:

"What! Was it from you that the Word of God first went forth? Or has it come to you only?" (1 Corinthians 14:36)

In this text, Paul seems to be saying, "What! Who do you think you are, setting yourselves up as the sole proclaimers of God's Word when what you're saying contradicts the Word of God?"

Both of the above interpretations are feasible. And both are in harmony with the rest of New Testament teaching. Namely, that women may speak in the house of God.

What kind of "teaching" is this?

Let's now turn our attention to the other "limiting passage." Before we look at the text, it's important to understand that 1st and 2nd Timothy are unique letters. Paul is writing to his apostolic apprentice—a man he's known for about fifteen years. Such communication—between two closely-tied individuals—is known as "low context." This means that the author can assume an intimate knowledge of the reader's understanding of any particular statement he makes.

Let me unpack that.

Because Paul had a close relationship with Timothy, he could say things to him that he knew Timothy would understand. His statement had a particular context to it with which Timothy was familiar. Suppose, for instance, I wrote a letter to one of my co-workers. And in the letter I made a statement about "apostolic priority." Other people reading the letter would be lost as to what I was talking about. But my co-worker would be clear because we have had several in-person discussions about it.

In the same way, 1st and 2nd Timothy are very difficult letters to interpret because they are literally dripping with "low-context" statements—statements that have a context that only Paul and Timothy were privy to. Therefore, the best we can do is try to piece together the exact situation that Timothy faced in Ephesus. Linguistic and historical scholars have uncovered several facts that throw light on the passage we are considering. And it meshes nicely with what we can uncover by mirror-reading the letter.[2]

Putting all the facts together, the following scenario emerges: Paul's warning to the church in Ephesus was finally coming to pass. Five years earlier he forewarned the Ephesian elders that wolves would penetrate the church and draw disciples after themselves with perverse teachings (Acts 20:28-30). The wolves had appeared. So Paul exhorts a young Timothy to combat their perverse teachings (1 Tim. 1:3-7; 6:3-5). Since Timothy was well aware of the heresy, Paul didn't need to explain it in detail. However, it appears that it was a kind of proto-gnosticism.

---

[2] Mirror-reading is the process of reconstructing the historical situation of a New Testament letter by reading the author's response in the letter. The author's response "mirrors" the specific situation to which he is responding. In the words of F.F. Bruce, when reading the New Testament letters "we are in a position of people listening to one end of a telephone conversation; we have to infer what is being said at the other end in order to reconstruct the situation for ourselves." (*Answers to Questions*, Grand Rapids: Zondervan, 1972, p. 93)

Gnosticism was a heresy that appeared in the second century. The Gnostics taught that full salvation comes through special knowledge (*gnosis*) that only the initiated possess. What Timothy was battling in Ephesus appears to have been an extremely embryonic form of this heresy. (Paul seems to refer to the heresy when he says to Timothy, "Turn away from godless chatter and the opposing ideas of what is falsely called knowledge (Greek: *gnosis*—1 Timothy 6:20, NIV).

According to the false teaching, both eating meat and engaging in marriage were forbidden (1 Timothy 4:1-3). Myths about the Law were also embraced (1 Timothy 1:4-7). We know from historical records that the Gnostics perverted the creation account. Eve was regarded as both a mediator and redeemer figure.[3] She pre-existed Adam. Man came into existence because of woman, and he was given enlightenment through woman. Since Eve was the first to take a bite from the Tree of Knowledge, she was regarded as the bearer of special spiritual knowledge (*gnosis*).

It is for this reason that those who accepted this heresy preferred the leadership of women over that of men. The heresy taught that women could still lead people to the illuminating *gnosis* that was represented by the Tree of Knowledge. It was further believed that redemption completely reversed the effects of the fall so that men were no longer subject to earthly authorities and women were no longer subject to their husbands.

While male teachers were spreading this doctrine (1 Timothy 1:20; 2 Timothy 2:17), it found fertile ground among the women in the church (2 Timothy 3:6-9). Worse still, their homes provided a network by which the false teaching spread rapidly (1 Timothy 5:13-15; 3:11). Add to that, the main religion in Ephesus was a female-only cult. The

---
[3] Compare this idea with Paul's statement in 1 Timothy 2:5.

priests who served the temple of Artemis (Diana) were all female. They ruled the religion and kept their men under their subjection. This mindset and influence appears to have crept into the Ephesian church. As a result, some of the women were acting bossy and seizing control over the men. They adopted the heresy and the attitude that goes along with it. And they began to peddle it in the church meetings. In short, the women were trying to take over the church with a false doctrine. This, I believe, is what provoked Paul to write the following passage:

> *"Let a woman learn in silence with full submission. I permit no woman to teach or to have authority over a man; she is to keep silent. For Adam was formed first, then Eve; and Adam was not deceived, but the woman was deceived and become a transgressor."* (1 Timothy 2:11-14, NRSV)

It's striking to discover that there are seven parallel words that appear in both this text and 1 Corinthians 14:34-35. Two of them are: learn and silent. In both passages, the word "learn" is translated from the same Greek word *manthano*.

> *"A woman should learn* (manthano) *in silence and full submission."* (1 Timothy 2:11)

> *"And if they desire to learn* (manthano) *anything, let them ask their own husbands at home."* (1 Corinthians 14:35)

In the Timothy passage, Paul says that the sisters in Ephesus should learn in silence and full submission. Why? Because they were being deceived by a false teaching.

The Greek word for silence in this passage is *hesuchia* and it means a temporary quietness, as in yielding the floor to let someone else speak. It also has the flavor of listening with studious attention. It's the same word that's used in Acts 22:2: *"When they heard him [Paul] speak to them in Aramaic, they became very quiet (hesuchia)."*

In effect, 1 Timothy 2:11 is the same instruction that Paul appears to give the sisters in Corinth. That is, the women ought not to disrupt the meeting with questions and challenges. In the church meeting, they should learn in quietness. So the first thing Paul says to Timothy is, "Let the sisters stop asking leading questions to challenge the brothers. Instead, let them take on humility and learn with studious attention."

But then, Paul builds on this point and says that the sisters are not to teach the brothers (1 Timothy 2:12). The original Greek is illuminating. It's in the present active voice. For that reason, it can be translated as: *"I am not now permitting a woman to teach."* New Testament scholar Ben Witherington writes,

> "In our study of 1 Tim 2.8-15, we find no universal prohibition of women speaking in church, but a dealing with serious problems that caused the author to ban women from teaching and domineering men in Ephesus. We conjecture that this was a response to women being involved in false teaching and being lead astray into apostasy . . . There is nothing in this material that suggests a permanent ban on women engaging in the ministry of the word."[4]

---

[4] For details, see Ben Witherington's *Women in the Earliest Churches* (New York: Cambridge University Press, 1988), chapter 3.

Consequently, Paul is not drafting a universal rule for women. Instead, he's dealing with a highly specific situation in Ephesus. He's speaking to those women in Ephesus who are peddling a false doctrine. As a result, Paul felt that they have forfeited their right to speak in the meetings.

Here is something else to consider. Timothy had known Paul for around fifteen years. Timothy had traveled with the aged apostle on two church planting trips.[5] He had also visited all the churches Paul founded. If Paul had universally banned women from teaching and speaking in the church meetings, why on earth would he have to explain this to Timothy in this letter? Timothy would have already known it.

Hmmm ...

But there's more. Paul goes on to say that no woman in the church is to "have authority over a man." The Greek verb translated "have authority" (or "usurp authority" as it stands in the KJV) is *authenteo*. Significantly, Paul didn't use the garden-variety word for authority (*exousia*) that he uses in his other epistles. *Authenteo* is an obscure term. The best authorities say that it can either mean "to exercise authority over" or "to seize authority over." Given the context, the second meaning is to be favored: "To seize authority over."[6] The women in Ephesus were trying to dominate the men. And Paul stood against it.

---

[5] See Frank Viola's *The Untold Story of the New Testament Church* for the historical background of Paul's entire ministry.

[6] See Louw and Nida's *Greek-English Lexicon of the New Testament Based on Semantic Domains*. They argue it means "to control in a domineering way ... to dominate men." Also see BAGD lexicon. Young's Literal Translation translates this phrase as "nor to rule a husband." Ben Witherington suggests it means to "rule over," "master," or "play the despot" over men.

After Paul instructs Timothy that the women can no longer teach in the church, he takes dead aim at the content of the heresy: *"For Adam was formed first, then Eve. And Adam was not the one deceived; it was the woman who was deceived and became a sinner."* (1 Timothy 2:13-14) Here Paul makes plain that Eve did not pre-exist Adam. He also states that it was Eve who was blameworthy. It was she who was deceived— just like the women in Ephesus. In all of Paul's other writings he always hangs the fall around Adam's neck. But given this particular situation, he sets his sights on Eve. And by doing so, he blows to bits the false teaching that some Ephesian sisters were promoting.

Repeat: Paul couldn't have been grounding a universal rule that forbade all women everywhere from teaching in the church meetings. This would contradict his own words. Consider the following:

> In 1 Corinthians, Paul states numerous times that women may prophesy in the church (1 Cor. 11:5; 14:26, 31). Prophecy contains instruction, for Paul writes, *"for you can all prophesy in turn so that everyone may be instructed (taught) and encouraged"* (1 Cor. 14:31).

> All Christians, including the women, are to teach and admonish one another through psalms, hymns, and spiritual songs (Colossians 3:16).

> The manifestation of the Holy Spirit, which includes prophecy, words of knowledge, and words of wisdom, is given to the whole church for the common good (1 Corinthians 12:1-12). And these gifts are to function in the church meetings (1 Corinthians 14). God bestows all spiritual gifts with undistinguishing regard on

men and women alike. There's no such thing as a gender-specific spiritual gift.

The author of Hebrews tells the whole church, including the sisters, that given their relative spiritual age, they all should be teachers (Hebrews 5:14).

The author of Hebrews also encourages the whole assembly, brothers and sisters, to exhort one another when the church gathers (Hebrews. 10:24-25).

Again, 1 Timothy 2:12 shouldn't be taken as a blanket statement that women may never minister in the church when men are present. To believe this would contradict the New Testament. Sisters would then have to cease from prophesying, exhorting, testifying, and operating in spiritual gifts—the things that Paul encourages. The overall context of 1 Timothy indicates that a false teaching was afoot and some of the sisters in Ephesus were pushing it.

I think Eugene Peterson rightly captures the flavor of Paul's message in this passage. He also throws light on verse 15—which is one of the most perplexing texts in the entire New Testament:

> "I don't welcome women to take over and tell the men what to do. They should study to be quiet and obedient along with everyone else. Adam was made first, then Eve; woman was deceived first—our pioneer in sin!—with Adam right on her heels. On the other hand, her childbearing brought about salvation, reversing Eve. But this salvation only comes to those who continue in faith,

love, holiness, gathering it all into maturity. You can depend on this." (The Message)

The real issue in both 1 Corinthians 14 and 1 Timothy 2 is the abuse of a God-given privilege. In both Corinth and Ephesus, Paul urges the sisters to give way to the brothers in the area of learning. Why? Because in Corinth, they were interrupting the meetings due to their lack of spiritual maturity and education. In Ephesus, they were brazenly seizing authority over the men with a false doctrine.

But the genius of Paul's instruction is that the women can learn. They should be tutored by their husbands at home so as to eventually be put on an equal social footing with the men. In this regard, Paul was a progressive thinker and a champion of a woman's honor in his day—a day when the notion of male superiority was well-entrenched.

Paul's arguments, therefore, have nothing to do with ministry. They rather have to do with order in the meetings. Paul is arguing for proper order where there exists disorder. He's issuing a corrective to, not a denial of, the public speaking of women.

In summary, Paul of Tarsus was called by God to liberate men and women from the bondage of the Law. Ironically, he's treated by some today as a new law-giver. The scribes of our Lord's day applied the Old Testament without any regard to local context. Tragically, scribalism is still with us. Modern scribes have turned New Testament verses into oppressive laws without any regard to local and temporary conditions.

By contrast, Paul's message is one that promotes radical freedom rather than suppression. And that freedom liberally extends to men and women. Therefore, if our interpretation of Paul contradicts his message of freedom, then we are connecting the dots incorrectly.

The bottom line

So where does this leave us? I can't speak for anyone else, but it leaves me here: The "zipper-position" which takes away a woman's right to speak in a church meeting reflects a very brittle approach to the New Testament. It's an unwarranted assumption that's based on a common, but culturally generated, misinterpretation of Paul.

The truth is that women are no less vital a part of the church than are men. Men are in dire need of women to show them Christ. (Keep in mind that the church—the *ekklesia*—is a female.) In addition, unlike the situation in the first century, women in our time are well educated. They are not our social inferiors.

Therefore, Paul's injunctions in the "limiting passages" only apply to women who are disrupting the church meetings by uninformed and disruptive questions. They also apply to women who are spreading false doctrines or seizing authority over men. In that light, consider this weighty text of Scripture:

> *"As it is, there are many parts, but one body. The eye cannot say to the hand, 'I don't need you!' And the head cannot say to the feet, 'I don't need you!' On the contrary, those parts of the body that seem to be weaker are indispensable, and the parts that we think are less honorable we treat with special honor. And the parts that are unpresentable are treated with special modesty, while our presentable parts need no special treatment. But God has combined the*

members of the body and has given greater honor to the parts that lacked it, so that there should be no division in the body, but that its parts should have equal concern for each other." (1 Corinthians 12:20-25, NIV)

To exclude women from functioning in the church gatherings is to resurrect the clergy system in new garb. The men become the new clergy caste. Only men are worth a hearing. The women become the new laity caste. What they have to say isn't as valuable. In fact, it's not valuable enough to even be heard. So they are closed off from functioning in God's house.

At bottom, if we give only men the right to speak in the gathering, we have unwittingly re-established the clergy-laity dichotomy. "One anothering" goes out the window. The old leaven of authoritarianism is dressed in new clothing. And all our rhetoric about restoring the priesthood of all believers devolves into just that—rhetoric. To call for fully participatory meetings, but only permit the males to speak is grossly inconsistent.

The Lord Jesus Christ is the sole mediator between the human race and God. In mediating us to God, He has established a new priesthood. And that priesthood includes both women and men. It would have been highly convenient for Paul to install some kind of restricted order of priests to water down a woman's high calling as Christ's kin. Sadly, the Lord's followers took that path rather quickly. But Paul himself refused to do so.

This is pretty diffuse, but I hope you get my drift: The New Covenant makes all of us priests, and Body life (which includes open-participatory church meetings) is the practical expression of that shared priesthood.

To put it in a sentence: *Breaching the main thrust of the New Covenant and the entire message of Scripture on the basis of two obscure passages has the tragic side effect of creating a male clergy caste.* Because the sisters are part of the royal priesthood (to borrow Peter's phrase), the New Testament invites them to testify, instruct, exhort, prophesy, sing, and pray in the meetings of the church (1 Corinthians 11:5; 14:26, 31; Colossians 3:16; Hebrews 10:24-25). The sisters are free to open their mouths and feed their fellow brethren with Christ. In so doing, they glorify God and help build the church.

So dear sister, I implore you: We need your part in the church meetings. We need your unique contribution whenever we gather. We need the texture of your personality as you share Jesus Christ with us. We need your wisdom, your good sense, and your unique insight. We need the fragrance of Christ that you so beautifully emit.

To muzzle you is to mute half the priesthood. It's to cause a major part of Christ's Body to become paralyzed. The meetings of the church are the natural outflow of the spiritual experience of each Christian. To deprive you from participating in this outflow is to bottle you up. It's to suppress your spirit. To deny you the right to function is to suggest that you do not hear from God. To silence you in the gathering is contrary to the very fiber of the church.

What about wives submitting to their husbands?

Once this chapter is published, some "which-side-are-you-on" consumers will hopelessly demarcate me into a warring camp.

Unfortunately, hornets cannot be prevented from buzzing. But if the truth be told, I don't fit neatly into any category. I'm neither a touchy-feely "Christian-feminist" nor a slashy-burny "patriarchal traditionalist."

Alert: May the extremists on both sides prepare to descend into grunts.

As far as the marital relationship goes, the husband/wife relationship is an earthly picture of the heavenly reality of Christ and His Bride. So I take at face value Paul's injunction for wives to be subject to their husbands (Ephesians 5:22: Colossians 3:18; see also 1 Peter 3:1-7). Yet I'm quick to add that this passage has been all-too often lifted out of its proper context and misused by controlling husbands who wish to brow-beat their wives. In addition, Paul is a strong proponent of Christians submitting to one another in the fear of Christ (Ephesians 5:21). Therefore, in a sense, husbands must also submit to their wives.

Jesus Christ doesn't dominate nor subjugate His Bride. Male domination of women, therefore, is a symptom of man's fallen nature (Genesis 3:16). It's not a Divine mandate. Yet submission and subjugation are two very different things.

I drone on. Hopefully, somewhere in this lengthy epistle you've found an answer to your question. I trust that my other sisters in Christ who read it will find within these words liberty and freedom from religious suppression.

Perhaps more rounds are needed, but this is all I have time for at the moment. Maybe someday I'll try to redress the deficiencies. So please accept it in that vein: It's a stab at something, not a finished product.

Your brother in the costly but glorious quest,[7]

Frank

Frank Viola is a Christian author and speaker. His public speaking covers a wide range of topics including the all-sufficiency of Jesus Christ, the deepening of the spiritual life, Christian community, church planting, God's eternal purpose, mission, and church restoration. He has written numerous books on the deeper Christian life and radical church reform, including the bestsellers From Eternity to Here *and* Pagan Christianity *(co-authored with George Barna) as well as* Finding Organic Church, Reimagining Church, Bethany, *and* The Untold Story of the New Testament Church. *His website is www.FrankViola.com.*

---

[7] For further information, see Ben Witherington's *Women in the Earliest Churches and Women in the Ministry of Jesus*, chapter 17 of F.F. Bruce's *A Mind for What Matters*, and N.T. Wright's *Paul for Everyone* series (1 Corinthians and The Pastoral Letters). To my mind, Bruce, Witherington, and Wright are among the greatest New Testament scholars this century has produced.

Wikiklesia Volume 2 Taking Flight

Change is in the Wind: Taking Flight

Cynthia La Grou

As we enter a new decade our heads are still spinning from the results of the last. There are few institutions and industries that are not navigating complex technological, cultural, and economic turbulence occurring the world over. Will it be survival of the fittest, the most informed, the most social, or the most innovative? One thing is certain, the winds of change are such a constant that the dust may never settle. Agility is key. The church is no exception—an exciting reformation and revolution is well under way. At the same time – there is nothing new under the sun. In reality, human nature *is* the constant that never seems to change.

In his book *Why Not Women?*, David Hamilton depicts classic human nature at work during Jesus' time, "In Luke 13:10-17, we read about the day Jesus was teaching in a synagogue when he spotted a crippled woman, bent over double. Jesus called her forward. When He laid hands on her, she immediately stood up straight, completely healed."[1] He notes that:

> *By Jesus' day women had been completely marginalized in places of worship. They were segregated into a separate*

---

[1] Lorin Cunningham and David Joel Hamilton, *Why Not Women?: A Fresh Look at Scripture on Women in Missions, Ministry and Leadership*, YWAM Publishing, 2000, 116.

court even though this was not part of God's original design for the tabernacle, nor was it the case in Solomon's temple, nor in the temple rebuilt by the exiles returning from Babylon.[2] By the second century after Christ, archaeology suggests that the synagogues kept women in screened second-floor galleries that they entered by a back door. The rabbis decreed that a synagogue could be established whenever there was a quorum of ten men. Even though there was no basis in Scripture for this, they were sending a clear message to their women: 'You (quite literally!) do not count.'[3]

Jesus' invitation stuck out against the male monopoly of public worship. When Jesus put [the crippled woman] in the spotlight, in front of the whole synagogue, He shattered the men's worldview. Jesus defended Himself by saying that this "daughter of Abraham" deserved to be released from her affliction, even on the Sabbath. Nowhere in rabbinical teaching was an individual woman called "a daughter of Abraham." Jewish men were often referred to as "sons of Abraham," but never a woman. (The Greek word anthropos *used in the phrase "Son of Man" is a gender-inclusive word.) Everyone knew that women weren't heirs of Abraham in the way that men were. But Jesus lavished this term on a woman. There was another reason the woman stood straight and tall that day in the synagogue. Jesus had done more than heal her back. He had restored her dignity as a person, showing her that she*

---

2 Ibid. 105

3 Ibid. 116

was valued by God. She was an equal heir with her male counterparts to all that God had promised Abraham.[4]

Such monopolies and screened partitions still exist. Regular announcements appear in my social media networks about groundbreaking missional conferences or initiatives. When I check them out, I often find a photo of 24 "founders," an initiative of 12 "history making" leaders, or a "missional" conference of 16 or more speakers—all men. I think, "How can these be considered 'missional' in an American culture that, for the most part, is better following Christ's example of inclusivity?" Each time a popular Christian magazine touting the "God - Life - Progressive Culture" comes in the mail, I thumb through the contents, scratch my head, and ask, "Is this a men's magazine?" A few years ago, I attended what I had considered to be the most progressive, thought-leading Christian leadership conference around. Coming from a secular professional background, I was shocked that the gender ratio in attendance was 5 to 70. Even though there is no basis in Scripture for this, the message is clear: "You, quite literally, do not count."

A plethora of thought on reimagined church structure and community is reshaping how we perceive fellowship, but all too often the superficial repackaging of entrenched hierarchal, top-down values and structures remains unchanged. We accept recalibrated structure, but still ignore deep biases and prejudices that become obstacles for moving into the future. One tell-tale sign of shallow repackaging is the lack of balanced gender representation. Even in the most groundbreaking, progressive religious scenes, women's contributions are neither encouraged nor fully acknowledged, while some of the more traditional denominations, such as Methodists and Wesleyans, have egalitarian views which are backed by practice. If it seems that the

---
4 Ibid. 116

current conversation is driven by men and that women do not participate, perhaps it because for centuries women have been disenfranchised by subtle and blatant messages of devaluation and exclusion.

The result is a continuing lack of inspiration and a dearth of role models for women in general. If role models for women leaders exist for the noble daughters of the future, where do we find them? Young women, in particular are steeped with stereotypical archetypes amply supplied by the culture and entertainment industry, most of which glamorize women as having low IQs and high sex-Qs. In sweeping terms, this low view of women feeds abusive attitudes and fuels demand in exploitive industries such as porn and trafficking. One wonders why all of this is being swept under the rug by the church. The true archetypical nature of men and women, as God created them to share in His glory, seems to be hidden. The church shows little concern or interest in uncovering a balanced view and representation of gender for God's glory and for the benefit of humanity. It remains paralyzed by fear, victimization, skewed vision, and inauthenticity.

During this time of reimagining, no one has more questions than women. Not all women are content to conform to the status quo, play supportive roles, or take on cultural trappings. They are not necessarily asking questions about their faith—they are asking questions about their place in the church or asking if they even have a significant role to play. Many are asking from places of pain, repeated rejection, and marginalization. Most, however, see what's going on from a distance and simply choose to stay away.

Removing the roadblocks

Based on accumulated research, a global and cultural consensus is mounting that has the potential to exonerate women from centuries of oppression. Nicholas Kristof (Pulitzer Prize-winning author and *NYT* columnist) and Sheryl WuDunn, former *Times* reporters and authors of *Half the Sky: Turning Oppression into Opportunity for Women Worldwide*, see the treatment of women in developing countries as the great story and moral issue of this century. Greg Mortenson, 2009 Noble Peace Price Nominee and best selling author of the books *Three Cups of Tea: One Man's Mission to Promote Peace...One School at a Time* and *Stones into Schools: Promoting Peace with Books, Not Bombs, in Afghanistan and Pakistan*, asserts that women will become the solution to many of the world's most ethical and economically pressing problems.

Equality is not only morally right, it is pivotal to human progress and sustainable development. Economic growth continues to bolster gender equality, but it is still a drop in the bucket. None of the Millennium Development Goals[5,6,7] can be achieved without addressing deeply rooted gender inequality because each goal is directly or indirectly tied to women's equal rights. Most of the world's greatest humanitarian needs and horrific injustices involve the discrimination and exploitation of women. Violence, prostitution, maternal mortality, and trafficking for starters are not considered "feminist" or "women's issues," but humanitarian and human rights issues that deeply affect us all (see Appendix 1).

---

5 Gender and the Millennium Development Goals, http://archive.waccglobal.org/wacc/publications/media_development/2006_3/gender_and_the_millennium_development_goals

6 Gender Equality and the Millennium Development Goals, http://www.mdgender.net/goals/

7 MDG Goal: Promote gender equality and empower women: http://www.unicef.org/mdg/gender.html, http://www.allbusiness.com/professional-scientific/architectural-engineering/3953844-1.html

This mounting consensus is well aware that historically, hierarchical religious institutions and cultural belief systems have impeded women from realizing their God-given potential while unwittingly underpinning some of the most deeply entrenched of all human attitudes. Will the church make sincere efforts and adjustments within its basic value system, or will increased understanding and light shed on this issue intensify skepticism of the church? Will God's mission be shown as one of relationship and reconciliation toward our fellow man and woman, or as one of denunciation and alienation? If our combined identity in God's image remains concealed and fractured, conflicting messages for men and women will continue to pervade the cultural psyche and thwart our ability to make effective strides regarding the key humanitarian issues of our time.

A light hidden under a bushel cannot be seen and a city on the hill cannot be hidden. True light radiates with authenticity. It leads by example. If the church decides its task is to live out the story of reconciliation, justice, and mercy, yet continues to marginalize half of its constituency, then how can it realistically expect to achieve its goals? Values regarding freedom from oppression should start with the faith community and permeate society, not the other way around. To do this, I propose a radical shift from theory to practice. Through its existing belief systems (see Appendix 2) the church can be reactionary and resist winds of change, it can be neutral until an overall consensus is reached, or it can recognize a vast ocean of untapped potential and lead. One of the world's greatest unacknowledged human resources and promoters of spiritual and social transformation are women.

A word for women

I believe that each one of us, regardless of gender, is accountable to God for our gifts. Are we good stewards of them, or do we bury our gifts out of fear or belief that we have not received permission to use them?[8] Our lifetime is short and valuable and the world's needs are great; we cannot afford to waste time waiting for change before addressing many of the pressing needs within our community and world.

Women in the developed world can dream and achieve anything—from running for the highest office, becoming CEO of a Fortune 500 company, to being commanding officer of the NASA space station or space shuttle. It is time for women of faith to start tapping into their God-given potential. The opportunities are endless, but to take advantage of them women need to realize, create, and utilize three types of value: spiritual, social and economic. These translate into tangible spiritual, social, and economic capital:

> **Spiritual capital:** That which is cultivated and produced from the application of one's faith, Biblical principles, spiritual ethics, and virtues to all areas of life. Virtues include faith, hope, charity, courage, leadership, patience, discipline, perseverance, justice, compassion, forgiveness, gratitude, and humility.[9]
>
> **Social capital:** Refers to connections and relationships embedded in social structures or networks that enable people to collaborate or coordinate action to achieve mutually beneficial goals.

---

[8] Matthew 25:14-30

[9] Theodore Roosevelt Malloch, *Spiritual Enterprise: Doing Virtuous Business* (Encounter Books, 2008).

Economic capital: Refers to financial wealth, especially that used to start or maintain a business, and to the means to produce goods or services. Closely related to economic capital is **human capital** which refers to the skills, knowledge, and labor used to produce economic value.

Creating three types of value—the Virtuous Woman Business Model

Let's look at a few examples of women creating spiritual, social, and economic capital. My favorite model is the Virtuous Woman from Proverbs 31. Though the means of doing business has changed, her qualities remain the same. The virtuous woman is industrious and entrepreneurial. The fabric of her life is skillfully woven with personal, family, and social responsibility. She takes care of her family and household while maintaining the trust of her husband. She is resourceful and works unceasingly and diligently. She gets up early. She employs people to take care of her household because she has assumed multiple responsibilities. She treats her employees well and cares for them as part of her own family by clothing and housing them.

She is a property manager and has a real estate license. She is an agriculturalist—she considers a field and buys it to plant a vineyard. She is a business owner—she creates a product and finds a market for it. She establishes financial credibility that enhances her family's credibility and standard of living. Her industrious ventures have a double bottom line, enabling her to stretch out her hand to the poor. She has formed a global non-profit or established a 501c3 social venture in her community. She looks for opportunities to serve.

Through all of this she shows wisdom and kindness, and she laughs at adversity because she trusts and fears (regards) God. She isn't consumed with her looks and doesn't have time for the pervasive consumer mentality that requires conformity to the relentless cycle of fashion. She is always gorgeous (because she is not stressed out) and radiates peace and wisdom from within. She is respected by her family and her community. All of this gives her a charming and sophisticated quality. A woman who fears God will be praised. She does not build a platform or seek attention or notoriety but allows God to give her honor in due time.

Another example of women creating spiritual, social, and economic capital, not only for their time but for future generations, includes those in the historic anti-slavery movement. Thanks to Walden Media's extraordinary film *Amazing Grace* we've all heard of William Wilberforce who led the parliamentary campaign against the British slave trade. Wilberforce was a statesman-saint and humanitarian reformer whose significant contributions reshaped the political and social attitudes of the time by promoting concepts of social responsibility and action.

But has anyone heard of Hannah More, Elizabeth Heyrick, or Sarah Wedgwood?[10] Lest we forget and believe that credit for a social movement and its historical consequences belongs to one or a few political elite, let us consider the entire picture and look at those who are being omitted in the contemporary media representation. And then let's ask why.

Many historical African heroes, such as Nanny, Kofi, Cudjoe, Accompong, Bussa, Quamina, and others spearheaded the end of slavery

---

10 "The Women for Liberation", February 2007, http://www.surefish.co.uk/abolition/200207_women.htm

through various means, including historic slave revolts. Conservative estimates are that 20 million Africans died as a result of the slave trade, more than three times the number of people who died through the Jewish Holocaust.[11]

Much of the success of the overall campaign can be attributed to the leadership of women. They *were* the major innovators of national anti-slavery organizations in the 1820s. They did not seek or gain fame, but rather worked collectively. Their endeavor marked not only a change in the role of women in society, but the nature of the campaign as a whole. Activist George Thompson stated, "Where they existed, they did everything…In a word they formed the cement of the whole anti-slavery building—without their aid we never should have been united."[12]

When the Society for the Abolition of the Slave Trade was set up, it was an exclusively male organization. Some of the leaders of the movement, such as Wilberforce, were opposed to women being involved in the campaign. Wilberforce, deeply conservative when it came to challenging the existing political order and who advocated change through education and religion, was concerned that women wanted to go further than the abolition of the slave trade.[13],[14] Early women activists such as Anne Knight and Elizabeth Heyrick were in favor of the immediate abolition of slavery, whereas Wilberforce believed that the movement should concentrate on bringing an end to the slave trade with the abolition of enslavement and a gradual process leading to

---

11 "Known Facts about famed campaigner, William Wilberforce" http://blackukonline.com/index2.php?option=com_content&do_pdf=1&id=238, Clare Midgley, *Women Against Slavery: The British Campaigns 1780-1870* (Paperback - Jun 29, 1995)

12 "The Women for Liberation", February 2007, http://www.surefish.co.uk/abolition/200207_women.htm

13 Ibid Midgley

14 Spartacus Educational, "Society for the Abolition of the Slave Trade, Women's Anti-Slavery Associations" http://www.spartacus.schoolnet.co.uk/REslaveryW.htm

colonization. Although women were excluded from the leadership of the Society, records show that about 10% of the financial supporters of the organization were women. In some areas women made up over a quarter of all subscribers.

The Abolition of the Slave Trade Act of 1807 didn't address the plight of those men, women, and children who were already sold into slavery throughout Britain's dominions. This prompted Sharp, Thomas Clarkson (the movement's campaign founder and chief architect), and Thomas Fowell Buxton to form the Society for the Mitigation and Gradual Abolition of Slavery. In 1823, a new Anti-Slavery Society was formed whose members included Thomas Clarkson, Henry Brougham, William Wilberforce, and Thomas Fowell Buxton. Although women were allowed to be members they were excluded from leadership.

On April 8, 1825, a meeting took place at the home of Lucy Townsend in Birmingham to discuss the issue of the role of women in the anti-slavery movement. Townsend, Elizabeth Heyrick, Mary Lloyd, Sarah Wedgwood, Sophia Sturge, and other women formed what would later become the Female Society for Birmingham. The formation of other independent women's groups soon followed. By 1831, there were 73 women's organizations campaigning against slavery.

Wilberforce's fear that women would advocate a more radical strategy proved to be correct. In 1824, Elizabeth Heyrick published her pamphlet *Immediate, Not Gradual Abolition*, in which she passionately argued for the immediate emancipation of the slaves in the British colonies. This of course differed from the official policy of the Anti-Slavery Society. The leadership of the organization attempted to suppress the existence of this pamphlet and Wilberforce instructed the leader of the movement not to speak at women's anti-slavery societies.

Change is in the Wind Cynthia La Grou

In 1830, the Female Society for Birmingham submitted a resolution to the National Conference of the Anti-Slavery Society calling for the organization to campaign for an immediate end to slavery in the British colonies. In an attempt to persuade the male leadership to change its mind on this issue, the society threatened to withdraw its funding of the organization. The Female Society for Birmingham was one of the largest local society donors, and it also had great influence over the network of ladies associations which supplied over a fifth of all donations.

As a result of several of these women's networks campaigns, the Anti-Slavery Society agreed to drop the words "gradual abolition" from its title. It also agreed to support Sarah Wedgwood's plan for a new campaign to bring about immediate abolition. The Society finally won its fight in 1833 with Parliament passing the "Abolition of Slavery Act." This finally gave all slaves in the British Empire their freedom.[15]

Though relegated to the footnotes of history, this movement of women set a benchmark for all future activist movements, including those existing today. These abolitionists formed the first membership organization to campaign for political change, forming local groups and sending out newsletters to keep members updated on progress. Their bulletproof techniques included lobbying, celebrity endorsement, boycotts of slave harvest sugar, and moral exhortations through the use of images, icons, publishing, and investigative journalism. They understood and used inspiration to stir up social sentiment, saturate cultural awareness, and ultimately influence the political agenda. It took 20 years to change public opinion—and the law—regarding slavery. But once these early abolitionists became aware of their potential, they went on to secure the vote for women and further women's rights.

---

[15] Spartacus Educational, Women's Anti-Slavery Associations, http://www.spartacus.schoolnet.co.uk/REantislavery.htm

Sadly, almost 200 years later, similar dynamics are still taking place today. Only the situation is exponentially more dire. Slavery is now the third largest criminal activity on the planet, enslaving millions, mostly women and children. Why have we regressed? Why are we not outraged? Poverty and fatherlessness (there are over 143 million orphan's worldwide—the population size of Russia) perpetuate human trafficking, suffering, and injustice. Yet these issues are minuscule compared to what's around the corner if we do not awaken and choose action now. Where is the army of women who feel strongly enough about injustice and oppression to make a difference? If the early abolitionist women saw both the current breadth of global slavery and the speed of the Internet to virally transmit a campaign, they would go ballistic. These Quaker women, despite heavy domestic responsibilities, found time to initiate and be responsible for a number of vitally important national initiatives of their time, while raising public awareness and creating global inroads towards justice and human equality.

Today we live in a leadership void. Women have the ability to inspire great ethical leadership as well as become great leaders. This ability has not gone unrecognized—a glance at the archetypical symbols attributed to women demonstrate their value: liberty, justice, wisdom (to be desired above riches and sought after above all else), and the church. Also, the Lady Liberty, symbol of freedom and democracy, is not standing still in the harbor, she is on the move. Her right foot is raised as her left foot tramples broken shackles at her feet, symbolizing the United States' commitment to be free from oppression and tyranny. But as long as inequality of any type exists, the true expressions of liberty, justice, wisdom, and the church will not prevail in authority or succeed in influence.

Women have explosive potential at this time in history

Women are realizing that their latent gifts and callings must find expression. Let the journey begin! But let it take root in places of fertile soil where people believe in you and are engaging and supportive. Quite simply, your dreams will never take root in an unsupportive environment. Few things will influence your success more than the people you surround yourself with.

If your gender is seen as a deficit rather than an asset, it may be time to reevaluate your environment. If your vision does not have wings, or if you do not have a voice in a particular environment, that is the first indication that you are expected to play a secondary or supportive role. Likewise, if you are not called to lead during this chapter in your life, make sure your values are aligned with your team and that your supportive role is appreciated. If you are appreciated, then your voice will be valued and heard in either situation.

Did you know that you have been designed to fulfill a personal calling? You can find challenge, adventure, and chart your own flight path. Books and online resources are available for you to obtain the equivalent of an MBA. Knowledge is not only at your fingertips, you also can connect with the people producing it. In some cases the degree you received 5-10 years ago could be obsolete given current technological and socio-economic trends. More than ever future leaders will self-educate, continuously replenishing their knowledge. You can form a group with those of similar dreams and passions, and that group can become a tribe, and that tribe can become a creative force, a movement, or a key part of a movement already in progress.

Did you know that the movements started today will become the marketplace of tomorrow? Within 8-10 years most businesses will have a social or environmental mission or a double/triple bottom line. According to research, women are much more likely than men to want to start a business with a social objective. Surveys show that nearly 50% of women want to use their "big" idea to help people less fortunate than themselves.[16] Men set up standards of currency for status that can be calculated by measurable performance. Women typically do not need measurable performance, but are comfortable with ambiguity. They tend to rate profit-maximizing below other holistic community, family, and personal values. Since recognition is not a priority, they promote themselves as a group rather than individually. Their leadership styles are naturally adaptive to the non-hierarchical landscape of the web.

Due to lingering pay unfairness and gender inequality in corporate America, women are taking flight by starting new businesses at twice the average rate of men. According to the Center for Women's Business Research, as of 2008, 10.1 million firms are owned by women (75% or more), employing more than 13 million people, and generating $1.9 trillion in sales. Experts predict that as women continue to gain in the current economy's growing industries, they will soon outnumber men in the work force. Women are now poised to drive the post-recession world economy thanks to an estimated $5 trillion in female-earned income that will be coming online over the next five years.[17]

Research also shows there is a strong correlation between how well top corporations develop and promote women leaders and how successful those corporations are in the marketplace. If companies lag

---

16 Colin Williams, "Mapping The Prevalence of Social Entrepreneurs: Promoting Social Entrepreneurship May Be a Key..." http://www.allbusiness.com/professional-scientific/architectural-engineering/3953844-1.html

17 Rana Poroohar and Susan H Greenberg, "Working Women are Poised to become the biggest economic engine the world has ever known", *Newsweek*, November 2009.

behind when it comes to utilizing talented women, they could be at a big disadvantage compared to their peers and competitors. One big reason for this is that women are their biggest customers, accounting for the majority of consumer purchase decisions in our consumer-oriented economy[18] where women control 83% of the spending in the US and $12 trillion of the global $18.4 trillion in annual consumer spending, which is expected to rise.

Based on their heartfelt passions and values, women have the collective spending power to make a difference. They can have a voice in how resources are spent in their church merely through their giving. Eighty-five percent of church resources go to maintaining overhead and top down programs, whereas two cents of every dollar goes to support global missions.[19] Opportunities are readily available to invest in women struggling with poverty through microfinance, for example, or to help children who are trafficked or who live in trash dumps in developing countries, as opposed to perpetuating high overhead with church building programs or new mega sound systems.

Future church

As we can see from the statistics above, the church is being turned inside out. It will become less about maintaining overhead, image, or the sermon, and more about living stories of participatory faith shared through local community and house church movements, combined with online activity through a global, interconnected conversation.

---

18 Olivia Pulsinelli, *Business Review West*, "Inforum's 2009 Women's Leadership Index shows gender diversity still lacking" http://www.mlive.com/business/west-michigan/index.ssf/2009/10/inforums_womens_leadership_ind.html

19 http://www.generousgiving.org/stats

Faith is not exclusively confined within the four walls of the church; believers are living out their faith in all areas of life. This includes how they create and spend spiritual and social capital that will benefit others.

Church in all its variations could become a more horizontal, collaborative platform for service, action, compassion, advocacy, community, and creation care. This "missional frontier" has many aspects including organic, house church, and community outreach through service, with "missional enterprise" (same as social enterprise/non profits). The church would have the opportunity to learn to become servants, not masters, better listeners and prayers than orators or performers. In so doing, it could more resemble the early church "movement," which was flexible and informal, with no clergy or gender distinctions, and which naturally presented significant roles to the women who helped shape the early Christian movement.

The church of the future will promote God's mission of reconciliation and forgiveness. Ideally, it will present a balanced image of God as both father and mother—a dual image which is both stern and unwavering, valuing corrective retribution for the oppressor, yet offering mercy, forgiveness, healing, and education for the underserved, the broken, the fatherless, and the oppressed. Because of their marginalized status women can have a greater understanding and opportunity to serve missionally and relationally.

When leadership is referred to in even the most progressive churches, it is typically assumed that it is male leadership. We are standing at a critical crossroads. Will the church equip younger generations of women to fulfill their calling to serve the overwhelming needs of a present era that increasingly values and expects gender inclusivity? Or will women continue to be systemically excluded? Likewise, will women, despite lack of support, affirmation, and recognition, be awakened by virtue and compassion to courageously choose to take flight into new missional frontiers as well as create value rich "virtuous women" enterprises?

Based on my own experience pursuing the latter, my walk with Christ has never been deeper or more meaningful and full of adventure. I have "true brothers," close male partnerships, which have been deeply enriching and supportive. They have come along side me (and I them), and have invested in the vision I represent. We are a horizontal team, each growing in skills and abilities, fulfilling our mission.

Because the church may not be in an immediate position to transcend its structural biases, I have reason to suspect that balanced supportive environments originating outside the traditional church will be extended to accommodate women of faith whose callings are finding expression. It is my hope and dream, on behalf of the virtuous daughters of the future, that woman's gifts and wisdom will not only fit naturally into the changing landscape of the faith community, but that women of faith will realize their spiritual, social, and economic potential to break new ground as well as revolutionize history and their place in it.

Cynthia is Founding Director of Compathos.tv, a non profit media foundation and creative community of pro and award-winning media partners who are passionate about creating results-oriented media campaigns delivering impact and viewer action, and which focuses its resources on non-profit initiatives around the planet, and she is a founder at Compathos Productions.

Cynthia is a creative professional with design experience in digital media, brand architecture, film, photography, web development, 3D animation, illustration, architectural, interior, landscape design, and more. She is Creative Director and Founding Partner with her husband John at Millennia Media Group, a suite of companies in the professional audio, recording arts and design industries.

She is also lead editor for Taking Flight *(Volume Two of The Wikiklesia Project) and was a contributing author and cover designer for Voices of the* Virtual World *(Volume One of the Wikiklesia Project).*

Wikiklesia Volume 2 Taking Flight
Women of the Kingdom
Felicity Dale

In 1983, my husband Tony and I had the opportunity to visit Dr. Paul Yonggi Cho's church in Seoul, South Korea. At that time, his church was the largest in the world at 350,000 members. One morning, shortly after our arrival, we were wandering through the administrative building and, much to our surprise, were offered a personal interview with Dr. Cho himself. During our twenty-minute conversation, perhaps the most memorable thing he said to us was, "You will never see a move of God in the West until you find merit in the women."

Christendom has long been patriarchal in nature, particularly here in the West. Women have been relegated to lesser roles within the church for centuries. For the most part, I don't believe this is deliberate misogyny these days. All of us, both men and women, have been trying to follow the Scriptures—and they apparently limit the role of women within the church.

For years, back in the UK, I was told that I could exert leadership in the church as long as it was done through my husband. I was led to believe that the only reason women ever led in a situation was because God couldn't find a man to do the job. I believed that I was equal but that my role was different (and lesser than) that of a man. For years I submitted to this teaching. I would like to tell you that it was a willing submission, but that would not be true. Tony would go off to leaders' weekends, which by definition were men-only events, leaving me with kids and diapers, and would come back totally blessed. I loved being with the kids, and I was thrilled that he was blessed, but I did mind being excluded from "where God was really moving and where all the action was" because I was a woman.

God has given me desires and gifts of strategic thinking. I love listening to God, particularly in the context of a group seeking to join Him in his work within the Kingdom. As a physician, I am capable of making life-and-death decisions, but for years I was not allowed to take any kind of leadership role in church because of my gender. This was a huge source of frustration and sadness for me.

Fast forward a number of years—we had moved from the UK to the United States. When we became involved with the simple/organic/house church movement here, there were no barriers to women doing anything God called them to, but I still occasionally hit situations where my gender was an issue.

For example, two years ago, my husband Tony and I were wakened by an early morning call on his cell phone. It was someone in the publishing business wanting to discuss the business side of a book I have written. "Can you put him on speaker phone? I'd like to hear what he has to say," I said.

Tony and the person chatted for a while and then the person on the other end said, "Of course, we'll have both your names on the cover. This book is far too important to have been written by a woman!"

It was at this point that I lost my sanctification. I didn't mind so much that the book was to be written in both our names—Tony and I have written books together before. It was the assumption that women could not do anything significant that bothered me, because that has been the perception for centuries: when it comes to anything strategic in the church, it is the men who are important.

However, change is in the wind. There is currently a ground swell—a sense of the brooding of the Holy Spirit—over the topic of women in ministry. It's like the calm before the storm. I believe that very soon we are going to see a movement of women—not a radical feminist one reacting to the injustice of the past—but a movement of God's Holy Spirit freeing women into their destiny. We will see Galatians 3:28—"*There is no longer Jew or Gentile, slave or free, male or female. For you are all Christians – you are one in Christ Jesus*"—fulfilled in our lifetime. What might happen when the other half of God's army, the female warriors, begin to take their rightful place alongside the men to follow the Holy Spirit's strategy in the world?

Society today is speaking prophetically to the church: women are not limited in what they can do. They are astronauts, physicians, politicians. Arguably one of the best prime ministers in recent British history was the "Iron Lady," Maggie Thatcher, who many people would say rescued the nation. The church is lagging behind society in its attitude towards women. Obviously this is a generalization; there are many wonderful exceptions. However, those who do not yet know Jesus are very unlikely to be attracted to a church that limits the role of women to making the coffee or running the children's ministry.

A parallel situation occurred over a century ago over the issue of slavery. Although Christians like William Wilberforce were at the forefront of the emancipation of slaves, some of the greatest opposition to the abolition of slavery also came from the church. Many of the most vocal Christians in those days were quite clear that the Bible supported slavery. After all, the Old Testament gives laws about it, Jesus mentions it without any apparent condemnation, and the apostle Paul discusses it in his letters—therefore it has to be something God approves of. Yet no Christian today believes that God approves of slavery, for the whole tenor of Scripture points towards liberty.

What was the role of women in the New Testament? Women played an important part in the ministry of Jesus. Some women traveled with him and helped to support his ministry (Mark 15:41; Luke 8:1-3). A woman anointed him for burial (Matthew 26:12). The women did not desert him at his crucifixion (Matthew 27:55). After his resurrection, the first people Jesus revealed himself to were not the disciples, but a group of women and he entrusted the message of his resurrection to them (Luke 24:1-11).

Jesus did not treat women as second-class citizens. Some of the most strategic conversations recorded in the Gospels are those of Jesus talking to women. These were not dumbed-down monologues. They were deep, theological discussions. Think, for example, of Jesus' conversation with the woman at the well in John 4, or his dialog about the resurrection with Martha in John 11. Jesus treated women as valued equals—in a day when most people regarded them as mere possessions.

Women were included in the gathering in the upper room after Jesus' ascension (Acts 1:14). Joel's prophecy in that context specifically mentions that the Holy Spirit will be poured out on both men and women and they will all prophesy (Acts 2:17-18). Phillip's four daughters were examples of this (Acts 21:9).

Phoebe was a valued minister in the church in Cenchrae, one whom Paul commended to the church in Rome (Romans 16:1). In fact, of the twenty-seven different named people in Rome mentioned in Romans 16, eight are women. Six of them are described as laboring in some way with Paul. One of them, Junia (verse 7), is even singled out as being an apostle. Her name has sometimes been changed to Junias, a man's name, but according to British theologian, Martin Scott, in his book about women, *For Such a Time As This*, Junia was a very common woman's name at that time. Quoting Lampe in *Word Biblical Commentary Series* by James Dunn, he states that there are over 250 contemporary references to Junia—not a single one to Junias.

What about women teaching? Priscilla and Aquila instructed Apollos in Ephesus (Acts 18:26), Priscilla's name being mentioned first in the original Greek manuscript. Actually, of the six times that Priscilla and Aquila are mentioned as a couple, in four of them she is named first—unusual in a time when women were often not even counted if the number in a crowd was being assessed (see Matthew 14:21). She may well have had the more dominant role of the two of them in the church. When Jesus chastised the church of Thyatira in Revelation 2, it was not because a woman was teaching, but because she was promoting immorality.

Our interpretation of Scripture has paralyzed half of the body of Christ. So what do we do with some of the verses that apparently limit women? Let's take a look at a few of them.

In Genesis 2:18, God says, "*I will make a helper fit for him* (Adam)." Women have long been told that this is their role—to be a helper for their husband, there to serve him. It is an enlightening exercise, however, to look at the other occasions on which this word "helper" is used. Of the twenty-one times the Hebrew word *ezer* is used, in all but six it refers to God. Typical examples include, *"I will lift up mine eyes unto the hills from whence comes my help. My help comes from the Lord, who made heaven and earth"* (Psalm 121:1,2), or *"Our help is in the name of the Lord who made heaven and earth"* (Psalm 124:8). The impression given is that *ezer* is a valued consultant brought in to assist where man is lacking, rather than some kind of divinely-appointed personal assistant.

How about the writings of Paul, most often quoted to prohibit the active role of women within the church? First Corinthians 14:34-35 is apparently quite clear:

> *"Women should be silent during the church meetings. It is not proper for them to speak. They should be submissive, just as the law says. If they have any questions to ask, let them ask their husbands at home, for it is improper for women to speak in church meetings."* (NLT)

These verses cannot be taken literally to mean that all women are to be silent in church, because earlier in chapter 11 women are told to pray and prophesy with their heads covered. So let's look at it more closely. In chapter 7, Paul states that he is answering questions the Corinthians have posed to him in a letter. He then goes on to discuss a number of differing situations, and chapter 14 is a part of this discourse.

There are actually three sets of people who are told to be silent (Greek *sigao*) in 1 Corinthians 14. In the other two situations, the problem is mentioned, they are told to be silent, and then a solution is given. The first occurs when someone wants to speak in a tongue without anyone present to interpret (verses 27 and 28). The solution is that they are to be silent and speak to God privately.

The second happens when more than one person has a prophecy (verses 29 and 30). The solution here is for the first person to be silent and the second deliver what God has given them.

However, in the verses about women, Paul doesn't describe the problem, perhaps because he thought it was obvious. Presumably some women were causing a disruption by asking questions in the meeting. Rather than cause a disruption, these women were to ask their husbands at home. No one assumes in either of the first two situations that the instruction to be silent was for every situation and for all time, but these verses on women have been used to keep them silent for centuries.

The other major passage that causes problems for women is found in 1 Timothy 2. Paul apparently does not permit women to teach or have authority over a man (verses 9-15). We don't have space in this chapter to dive too deep here, but clarity comes in the singular and plural uses of the word "woman." There are certain instructions given that apply to women (plural), but the challenging verses apply to a woman (singular). A good explanation would be that there was one particular woman who was causing problems with wrong teaching, and a description of some disciplinary action taken to stop her is described in this passage.[1] This is similar to the discipline prescribed for an unnamed man in 1 Corinthians 5.

If God does not permit women to lead and teach within the church, then what do we do with the incredible examples of women

---

[1] For further exploration of this passage, see Jon Zens' Web site at http://searchingtogether.org/free-to-function.htm

He is using around the world? What do we do with Heidi Baker who, with her husband Rolland, has seen over 10,000 churches start across Mozambique and the surrounding nations in Africa?[2] Or Michele Perry, who most people would have written off for active missions work because of a physical disability (she was born with only one leg)? She has an orphanage in war-torn Sudan with more than 100 orphans.[3] How about Tillie Burgin, a woman now in her seventies who runs Mission Arlington, a ministry to inner city Arlington, Texas, that now has 4,000 people in regular attendance in more than 250 groups or congregations?[4]

In nations like China, primarily women and teenagers have been responsible for the remarkable spread of the Gospel there. Recently we were in India, staying in the home of some people who lead a rapidly growing church planting movement. They introduced us to two young women, one of whom was responsible for planting 6,000 churches, and the other 2,000.

Within the simple church movement, God is using women in all kinds of ways. I am aware of several women who, perhaps because they are not perceived as a threat and because they are not out to build their own empires, He is using to coordinate things at a regional level, developing conferences and other regional resources.

However, women in strategic positions within the church—whether that is legacy or simple church—are, sadly, a small minority. The majority of leadership in the church is male. Most women who have been brought up in the church have been conditioned to accept they will follow the lead of a man when it comes to spiritual life.

---

[2] http://www.irismin.org/p/home.php

[3] http://www.iris-sudan.org/

[4] http://www.missionarlington.org/ourmission/2008Results/

Don't try this at home, but I am told that if you take fleas and put them in a container with a lid on they will at first attempt to jump high. But after hitting their little flea heads on the lid several times, they will limit themselves to jumping low. Even when the lid is removed, they still will not jump out of the container. They have become conditioned to doing less than they are capable of.

The same is true for women. Even though there are no longer barriers in as many churches, for so long we have limited ourselves that we do not know how to use our new freedom. We need the Lord to help us to break us out of our low inertia so that we can move into our destiny as women of the Kingdom.

What part can the men play in this? Several times over recent years as we've spoken on this subject, we have seen the Lord lead the men in a gathering to repent over the attitude of the church to women. Often with tears, they have confessed at a personal and corporate level the wrongs done to women, and then released them to go out and be everything God is calling them to be. These times have always been profoundly healing for the women involved.

My husband, Tony, has long been a champion of women. He is a very gifted communicator, but he came to realize that the only way I would speak out was if he kept quiet. For many husbands, the best way they will help their wives to contribute meaningfully and strategically is to willingly stand down and joyfully promote their wives' gifts. At first, the women will not do as well as the men would have done, but in the longer term this will allow women to take their rightful place as equal ministers alongside them in the Kingdom.

Women of the Kingdom Felicity Dale

God is using in remarkable ways some African-American friends of ours who have chosen service as their way of operating within the Kingdom. They have willingly embraced service to Jesus and His body. As women, we have many centuries of service in the body of Christ behind us. We could, as the Holy Spirit brings women into more prominence, demand our rights and militantly seize position or prominence as a reaction to the injustices of the past. I do not believe God will bless this. Let's humbly, and with a spirit of service to our Lord, move into whatever God chooses to bless us with.

The day of women in the Kingdom is approaching fast. We have seen how some men have approached leadership in the Church—competition and rivalry, lording over and putting down. Let's not go that route. Let's choose to die to our ambition and agendas. We don't want the limelight or the prominence. And let's serve Jesus with all our hearts alongside the men and see His Kingdom come.

For further reading, I recommend the following books:

Why not Women by Loren Cunningham and David Hamilton
For Such a Time as This by Martin Scott
10 Lies the Church Tells Women by J. Lee Grady
Woman: God's Plan not Man's Tradition by Joanne Krupp
The Fall of Patriarchy by Del Birkey

Felicity Dale received her medical training at Barts Hospital in London, and worked as a family doctor before leaving to look after her own family of four children. She and her husband, Tony, were active in the British House Church Movement, helping to pioneer a church in their medical college and later in the East End of London.

In 1987, the Dales moved to the United States where they developed businesses to support themselves, and again jumped heart-first into church planting. Out of these church planting pursuits, the vision and relationships developed that led to the formation of House2House Ministries (primarily a website that seeks to resource the rapidly growing house church movement in the West). Felicity has authored Getting Started *and* An Army of Ordinary People, *and, with Tony and George Barna, is co-author of* The Rabbit and the Elephant. *Check out www.house2house.com.*

change is

in the wind

"The day will come when men will recognize woman as his peer, not only at the fireside, but in councils of the nation. Then, and not until then, will there be the perfect comradeship, the ideal union between the sexes that shall result in the highest development of the race."
—— Frederick Douglass

Wikiklesia Volume 2 Taking Flight
Leadership Lenses, Jungian Archetypes, and Gender
Leonard Hjalmarson

When I met the Lord at the age of nineteen in 1976, I entered a church culture which had made a covenant with modernity. While that culture reigned, the pact was relatively transparent and mostly functional. Culture was a container, and the gospel was water: the water took on the shape of the container, largely uncritical of the way the container shaped the gospel itself.

This compromise worked until, changing metaphors abruptly, "someone moved the cheese." Then with increasingly rapid pace, the gospel and the culture—or really, our churches and the culture—moved apart. The distance and difference was rarely noticed except by those on the margins. But as the disconnect grew, it opened space for perspective, for critique of both church and culture, and hope for transformation.

* * *

My first encounter with the stance of a hierarchical and patriarchal system with regard to women came in a Bible school class in Winnipeg in 1979. The class was on the sociology of religion, and it became jarringly evident to me that women were co-equal in creation, but not co-equal in the church. While the meanings of various texts, principally in Timothy, were debated, I decided that the trajectory of Jesus teaching and similarly the trajectory of Paul's teaching were toward liberation and complete equality, and since that time I have sought to empower women.

Theologically, issues around church governance have become simple for me. I argue that the Spirit gifts men in the same way as He gifts women: He is Lord and we follow His lead. Therefore it isn't up to me to decide who has authority as a pastor or a prophet or a teacher in the assembly; it is a matter of discernment. When character and gifting combine, we can only say "Yes, Lord," and partner with His work among us, regardless of gender.

Leadership lenses and Saul's armor

In terms of leadership paradigms, it is often assumed that men, being driven by testosterone and competition, function most naturally in a hierarchical structure. One could defend this with the observation that in established and "inherited" churches—that is, church communities that operate with a command-and-control style of leadership—the senior leaders are nearly always male. But I think the question is really one of those "which is first, the chicken or the egg?" problems.

In modernity, our paradigms were hierarchical. Growing out of the industrial revolution, we evolved a "heroic" leadership style that was like a pyramid. Popular culture gave us Rambo, the Lone Ranger, and Superman. Naturally, we looked for command-and-control type leaders to fill those roles, and western white men were socialized to take charge.

Theologically this manifested in a functional monism. Christology and the connection to kingdom rule offered a paradigm for hierarchy and command-and-control models. The neglect of Trinitarian thought in modernity was not accidental, but another manifestation of our tendency toward reductionism. Michel de Certeau has demonstrated that the totalizing and universalizing tendencies of modernity and rationalism supported hierarchical models.[1] The Trinity, which legitimated something like social egalitarianism at worst and an entirely new social reality with no Jew or Greek, slave or free, male or female at best, was neglected.

No surprise then that we majored on Christology even as we structured our churches for command-and-control from the top down with the (male) senior pastor at the top.

Command-and-control worked for some men, but others of us were bent and twisted out of shape in order to work within that model. We felt like the suit never fit. Like David wearing Saul's armor, we felt lost in a foreign world. We wanted to invite collaboration, but that invitation was perceived as "weak leadership." We wanted to invite questions and discussion, but that was perceived as uncertainty or incompetency. And many men who were not hard drivers always feared being labeled "effeminate."

While the consequence of fitting round pegs into square holes is destructive to many men on a personal level, systemically there is a similar result. The modern church marginalized certain gifts, such as those bent toward collaboration, gifts that were primarily relationally-

---

[1] Douglas John Hall writes, "Christomonism and the exclusivity that attends it represents, I believe, a failure of trinitarian theology. For a triune understanding of God, the western tradition especially was always tempted to substitute an undialectical monotheism heavily informed by a christology emphasizing the divinity principle and downplaying Jesus' true humanity." *Confessing Christ in a Post-Christendom Context*, 1999. Strongly in the background of this discussion are questions of alterity, or "otherness," reflections found in the work of Miroslaw Volf, LeRon Schults, Brian Walsh and others.

oriented, and gifts that were poetic, prophetic, and highly pastoral. We evolved and preferred command-and-control to the organic and relational gifts preferred in the New Testament. In short, we not only embraced a patriarchal system, but also a modern and technocratic paradigm while avoiding a spiritual and relational one.

Jung's *anima and animus*

It would be easy at this point to look for a psychological system that could offer an alternate lens on these issues, and the one that pops into mind is the Jungian framework. Because Jung pervades so much popular thought, his influence is both transparent and powerful. Let's take a moment to review the basics.

Carl Gustav Jung was considerably less neurotic than Sigmund Freud, and also much more open to religious experience (Jung suggested that spirituality is the best cure for addiction). Jung gave us the concepts of the *anima and animus*—the unconscious or true inner-self of an individual, as opposed to the *persona* or outer-aspect of the personality. The male unconscious finds expression as a feminine inner personality—*anima;* likewise the female unconscious is expressed as a masculine inner personality—*animus.*

The male inner-self can be identified as the totality of his unconscious feminine qualities and the female inner-self as her unconscious masculine qualities. Jung stated that the *anima/animus* archetype was not totally unconscious, calling it "a little bit conscious and unconscious."[2] In an interview, he gave an example of a man who falls head over heels in love, only to regret later in life his blind choice as he finds that he has married his own *anima*—the unconscious idea

---
2 Belanger, Jeff and Dalley, Kirsten. *The Nightmare Encyclopedia: Your Darkest Dreams Interpreted,* Career Press, 2005.

of the feminine in his mind—rather than the woman herself. The *anima* is usually an aggregate of a man's mother, but may also incorporate aspects of sisters, aunts, and teachers.

The *anima* is one of the most significant autonomous complexes of all. It manifests itself as figures in dreams as well as by influencing a man's interactions with women and his attitudes toward them. The converse is true for females and the *animus*.

Jung believed *anima* development has four distinct levels in men, which he named *Eve, Helen, Mary*, and *Sophia*. In broad terms, *anima* development in a male is about the male subject opening up to emotionality, and consequently a broader spirituality, by creating a new conscious paradigm that includes intuitive processes, creativity and imagination, and psychic sensitivity towards himself and others where it might not have previously existed.

Jung focused more on the male's *anima* and wrote less about the female's *animus*. Jung believed that every woman has an analogous *animus*—a set of unconscious masculine attributes and potentials. He thought that there are four parallel levels of *animus* development in a female: *the athlete, the planner, the professor,* and *the guide.* He viewed the *animus* as being more complex than the *anima*, postulating that women have a host of *animus* images while the male *anima* consists only of one dominant image.[3]

Implications for anthropology

The utility of Jung's work on gender, and in particular around the unconscious and these mythical archetypes, is possibly the most

---
3 Jung, Carl. *The Psychology of the Unconscious,* Dvir Co., Ltd., Tel-Aviv, 1973 (originally 1917).

influential psychological/anthropological framework ever developed. But in what sense are they "true?" And secondly, if we accept them as representing gender reality at some level, what are the implications for anthropology—our fundamental view of what it means to be human and created in the image of God?

I will beg off the "truth" question with just a few short comments. No framework represents the whole truth, but only illuminates some aspect of it. While I would argue that the object relations theory that grew out of analytic psychology offers great help in developing therapeutic paradigms, it remains only another way of seeing "through a glass darkly." It is not final, or perfect, or conclusive in any foundational sense.

The "implications" question is more complex, and more important[4] and I have some questions and doubts about the Jungian framework.

To restate, according to Jung "the entire process of *anima* development is about the male subject opening up to emotionality, and in that way a broader spirituality, by creating a new conscious paradigm that includes intuitive processes, creativity and imagination."

It is not difficult to affirm that greater intuitive sensitivity, increased spirituality, or increased creativity are good things. But what worries me about this framework is that it implies a fundamental problem with our original design. In popular thought at least, to become more fully male is to embrace one's inner female. In other words, to

---

4 Coincidentally, David Fitch critiques the Jungian frame in his book, *The Great Giveaway* (Grand Rapids: Baker Books, 2005)

be fully male is to move psychically and spiritually toward the female. This implies that there is something lacking in maleness as created.[5] Secondarily, it implies that the qualities of sensitivity, intuition, and creativity are essentially non-male, but female qualities. This cannot be proved, any more than it can be proved that aggression is an essentially male, non-female quality.

Is there something lacking in the male gender as created? This kind of speculation is found as far back as Aristotle, who offered an analogy of incompleteness to explain the pervasive nature of romance. His ideal appears somewhat androgynous.

But what if something very different was true? What if sensitivity, intuition, and creativity were not gendered at all, but simply part of the *imago Dei*? Then to become more sensitive, compassionate, and creative is to become more fully human. To become more masculine, then, is not to embrace femininity, but *to embrace who we are*. Similarly for women, wholeness is not found in embracing neglected masculinity, but in finding her true self as created in Christ.[6]

I suspect that the popular frame of incompleteness and the need to embrace the *anima* or *animus* is at least partly apologetic. When we articulate the need for men to embrace the feminine, we hope to make men more open to women in general, to value, to welcome and embrace them for all the gifts they bring. But if we must do this by in some way moving men away from something essentially male, we risk alienating them from their essential selves.

---

[5] And by extension, we cannot view Jesus as a fully human male, but rather as an androgynous being.

[6] See in particular the work of Parker Palmer and his reflections in *A Hidden Wholeness* (San Francisco: Jossey-Bass, 2004).

What if, instead, there was a unique male mode of feeling just as there is a unique female mode? What if there was a unique male mode to all those things we identify as essentially feminine (masculine intuition, masculine creativity, masculine spirituality), and a unique female mode for the things we identify as essentially masculine? To me, the Jungian framework is an attempt to recover by theft what is ours by nature. As such, it offers as much distortion as it offers illumination, and I am not confident that it incorporates a biblical anthropology.

Leadership under a changing sky

Over the past few years my mentors in leadership and spirituality have embraced a holistic framework: Peter Senge, Margaret Wheatley, Peter Drucker, Len Sweet, Robert Clinton, Henri Nouwen, and Alan Roxburgh. By and large, these writers affirm that leadership is a communal task, and that the way forward is not found in command-and-control type frames, but in empowering all types of leadership in both genders. All these writers recognize that hierarchy is inefficient and destructive.

Two of the leadership definitions I like the best are offered by Gary Hamel and Peter Senge, respectively. Hamel writes, "Leadership is not defined by the exercise of power, but by the capacity to increase the sense of power among those who are led." Senge states (abbreviated), "Leadership is the capacity of a community to bring forth new realities."[7]

If there is a single metaphor that anchors this change in perspective, it is offered by Margaret Wheatley in an interview with

---

[7] Leadership is the capacity of the community to bring forth new realities. The leader is a designer (of the learning process), a steward (of the community vision and values) and a teacher (of the ability to learn and grow).

Larry Spears of the *Greenleaf Center for Servant-Leadership* in November, 2001:

> *Now more than ever, we have to fundamentally shift our ideas of what makes an effective leader. We have to shift them away from this secretive, command-and-control, "we know what's best." We have to leave all that behind, even though it may be effective in the moment . . . What I find in servant-leadership . . . is this fundamental respect for what it means to be human. And I think that right now the greatest need is to have faith in people. That is the single most courageous act of a leader. Give people resources, give them a sense of direction, give them a sense of their own power and just have tremendous faith that they'll figure it out.*

> *"We need to move from the leader as hero, to the leader as host. Can we be as welcoming, congenial, and invitational to the people who work with us as we would be if they were our guests at a party? Can we think of the leader as a convener of people? I am realizing that we can't do that if we don't have a fundamental and unshakable faith in people. You can't turn over power to people you don't trust. It just doesn't happen . . . I think one really needs to understand that we have no control, and that things that we have no control over can absolutely change our lives.*

One cannot speak about leadership in faith communities apart from the five-fold gifts of Ephesians 4. But neither can one merely talk about apostles, pastors, prophets, teachers and evangelists as if these words dropped from heaven. All these terms have become loaded with cultural meaning developed first in the Reformation and then anchored in practice largely bemired in modernity. We colonize words just like we colonize cultures. In order to use these words aright in the new world, we have to expand our field of vision. That field is largely gender-neutral, and it recognizes new leadership types.

Within the five traditional gifts, there are certain combinations that appear new and uniquely suited to times requiring innovation and adaptation: the *poet*, the *synergist*, and the *boundary-crosser*. These types are primarily a blend of prophetic and apostolic gifts.

The *poet* is especially oriented to helping us recover a missional imagination. The *synergist* is like an abbot figure. The *boundary-crosser* is a prophetic networker with pastor-at-large overtones. Alan Roxburgh describes the poet and the synergist in *The Sky is Falling*: "The poet, like Adam, helps us make sense of our experience. The word in the prologue of John tells how Jesus 'became flesh and lived among us.'"[8] In a similar way, the poet shapes words so that what was hidden and invisible becomes known. The poet removes the veil and gives language to what people are experiencing. This is only possible when the poet lives within the traditions and narratives of the people, "living reflexively in the traditions . . . The poet listens to the rhythms and meanings occurring beneath the surface."[9] But the poet also has a prophetic bent: "Poets immerse themselves in the multiple stories running beneath the surface of the culture . . . feel the power of these stories and critique their claims and pretensions on the basis of the memory and tradition of the community."[10]

---

8 Alan Roxburgh, *The Sky is Falling: Leaders Lost in Transition* (Eagle, ID: ACI Publishing, 2005) 166.

9 Ibid. 166

10 Ibid. 166

The leadership of poets, however, is not expressed in a modern manner:

> "[Poets] are not so much advice-givers as image and metaphor framers . . . What churches need are not more entrepreneurial leaders with wonderful plans for their congregation's life, but poets with the imagination and gifting to cultivate environments within which people might again understand how their traditional narratives apply to them today."[11]

Finally, Roxburgh notes that, "Poets make available a future that does not exist as yet; they are eschatologically oriented. From this environment, a missional imagination emerges."[12]

The synergist is an old role we need again, both to counter the fragmentation of modernity and to help us bridge the complexity we face at every level. Roxburgh writes that leadership groups must develop and work together across tribal lines. For this purpose we need what Roxburgh calls "the Abbot/Abbess," and what Lawrence Miller develops as the synergist:

> ". . . a leader with the capacity to unify diverse and divergent leadership styles around a common sense of missional vision for a specific community."[13]

> "[A synergist is] a leader who has escaped his or her own conditioned tendencies toward one style and

---
11 Ibid. 167
12 Ibid. 167
13 Ibid. 155

incorporated, appreciated and unified each of the styles of leadership on the life-cycle curve. The best managed companies are synergistic."

The synergist both embodies and guards the ethos, and her role is to foster and maintain a creative and open space within the team so that no one role dominates. The synergist is often a boundary-crosser, but I believe this gift exists outside the particular role as an expression of its own. A study from the University of Tasmania some years ago examined innovation and problem solving with sustained effect on communities. One outcome they found was an expanded lens for leadership and the discovery of a new (probably old) type of leadership: *boundary-crossers.*[14]

These people bridge certain groups and interests, they legitimize wider partnerships, and their interpersonal skills strengthen key relationships across boundaries. Interestingly, one of the key traits of these people, "is their ability to speak multiple languages" (the language of business and school in the Tasmania case.)[15]

So these people are edge-walkers, they speak multiple cultural languages, and we sometimes wonder if they are "in" or "out." But their function on the margins is critical to the life of our communities, helping to keep the boundaries permeable so that air can get in and life can flow out. I believe this role is especially needed when communities have been ghettoized and isolated for too long. As the systems theorists tell us: "Equilibrium is death." Boundary-crossers challenge the status

---

[14] This type appears in the work of Malcolm Gladwell as "the connector." *The Tipping Point* (London: Abacus, 2000) 51.

[15] Sue Kilpatrick, Ian Falk, Susan Johns, "Leadership for Dynamic Learning Communities," University of Tasmania Press, 2003.

quo indirectly by opening channels of growth and interaction on the margins.

Finally, Peter Senge and associates talk about how boundary-crossers enable accelerated learning, legitimizing wider partnerships. Culturally, and especially within the Church, we are off the map and in need of navigators and bridge builders, and we must find ways to harness the learning ability of entire tribes of people. I don't know anyone who has captured this need like Peter Senge:

> "In the knowledge era, we will finally have to surrender the myth of leaders as isolated heroes commanding their organizations from on high. Top-down directives, even when they are implemented, reinforce an environment of fear, distrust, and internal competitiveness that reduces collaboration and cooperation. They foster compliance instead of commitment, yet only genuine commitment can bring about the courage, imagination, patience, and perseverance necessary in a knowledge-creating organization. For those reasons, leadership in the future will be distributed among diverse individuals and teams who share responsibility for creating the organization's future."

If these teams fail to be gender-diverse, it is unlikely that they will birth the kind of leadership community that will enable us to move forward in these new places we find ourselves.

We might have expected in the past to see more women in roles requiring boundary crossing, collaboration, synergy, and new imagination. Perhaps indeed women will lead the way.[16] Women are more readily legitimated and approved for collaborative behavior, and much of the leadership we need will come from women. Men must be prepared to affirm leadership where we find it, regardless of gender. Yet perhaps that isn't stated quite strongly enough, because many of our sisters are reluctant to lead in a sub-culture that isn't sure whether to fully affirm women as leaders. Women will need more support than men in order to find their place among us: we must not fail to offer it.

Len is a writer, pastor, and software developer living among the orchards and vineyards of Kelowna, B.C. He is a regional representative for RESONATE, and was a contributor and editor of Voices of the Virtual World *(Volume One of The Wikiklesia Project). Len holds a D.Min in Leadership and Spirituality from ACTS Seminaries in Langley, B.C. Len is the Director of Spiritual Formation for FORGE Canada and is married to Betty, a registered nurse who works with women in transition. Len blogs at www.nextreformation.com and edits the Missional Voice journal at www.forgecanada.ca.*

---

16 I strongly agree with Sally Morgenthaler on this. Her article "Leadership in a Flattened World" is well worth the read. (See Pagitt and Jones, Eds. *An Emergent Manifesto of Hope*, (Grand Rapids: Baker Books, 2007).

Wikiklesia Volume 2 Taking Flight
Kingdom of God or Men?: Questions for Thinking Through Our Cultural Context
Brad Sargent

We are in the midst of a massive global change as cultures move away from division to inclusion, from a comprehensive set of separate parts to an interconnected system that is whole. We in the West also find ourselves in a flow of history that is post-Christendom, post-pragmatist, and post-feminist (among many other forms of post-somethingness).

These many changes could spur us to pull back and retreat like a tortoise into our shell. However, we would miss out on the opportunity to push forward into the future with confidence. Change is inevitable; transformation is volitional. If we choose to be transformed within our times, we will find ourselves in an era when gender relations in church and community could make substantial progress.

Truly, this is a *kairos* kind of moment that represents the "fullness of times" on issues of conflict and collaboration between men and women. To paraphrase 1 Chronicles 12:32, what must we consider to "understand the times and know what the Kingdom should do?" Before we can get to a deep discussion of what practical skills will be needed, we need to ask ourselves some critical questions about the paradigm in which we will practice.

Kingdom of God or of Men? Brad Sargent

Section one: What new space are we in, how did we get here, and what are the consequences and opportunities?

From the culture side of things

We live in a post-feminist world where those born after the battles for "women's liberation" and "women's rights" take it as a given that men and women are basically equal. We got to this place in history because, as psychologist Helen Haste writes,

> "In the long run, what counts is how the next generation thinks. How far new ideas permeate culture is not measured just by attitude change during one generation, but by what is taken for granted in the next."[1]

Ms. Haste used that statement to begin a chapter on "The Next Generation," whose members grew up not having to fight the social and political battles of the feminist movement in the 1960s and 1970s, but who inherited the benefits from those who did. Since these younger generations of women and men live in a country that views gender equality as a given, what does that mean for us in the Church?

Whether we approve the *content* of feminist worldviews and agendas or not, we've got to understand it because it is the *context* in which we live and serve. We have to deal with what is really there and not just with what we believe should ideally be there. If we don't choose to contextualize our Kingdom work for the real world, we shouldn't really complain when everyday people are repulsed by our presence

---
1 Haste, Helen, The *Sexual Metaphor: Men, Women, and the Thinking that Makes the Difference*, page 149

and/or presentation. We can't totally blame their responses on spiritual blindness when we prove to be culturally blind, can we?

From the church side of things

The theologically conservative wing of the Church is starting to see consequences of their "airbrushing women out of the Scriptures," as Bishop N.T. Wright so vividly calls it. As I perceive it, they simultaneously paint women into a corner when it comes to roles in family, community, and ministry. Meanwhile, the theologically liberal wing may appear to have conquered the issues of gender, but I think they are traditionally weak in other ways. For example, theological liberals struggle with cultural syncretism, in this case tending to adopt feminism uncritically. In reality, the underlying issues the church has are not about gender relations as much as they are about the modernist split that pits conservative and liberal interpretations against a holistic paradigm (more on that in section three).

What could be some consequences and opportunities?

I think it's worth sharing an extended excerpt (slightly edited) of a comment I made to a friend's blog post that referred to the aforementioned video of N.T. Wright:

> "In 4 minutes and 42 seconds of off-the-top speaking, Bishop Wright has exposed with both grace and subtlety a significant problem with internal theological consistency. The Christian traditions which theoretically emphasize inspiration and inerrancy often deny those same doctrines in practice when it comes to questions of women in ministry.

And, though I was reared in a liberal mainline tradition, theological conservatism is the stream I most identify with now, so I am attempting to be a friendly insider critic here. I've seen how our exegetes, theologians, and practitioners minimize or even "airbrush" women out of the biblical accounts, as Bishop Wright puts it, thereby explaining away what is clearly in the text. But such attempts to brush over, scratch out, or erase sections of the inspired text represent *eisegesis*, not intellectually consistent *exegesis*. They read our cultures into the text and change it, rather than letting the text read our cultures and change them by changing us.

"There are consequences to this bias against seeing the women who are right there in the New Testament texts, regardless of whether our bias finds its source in theological pride, intellectual weakness, personal privilege, the pursuit of power, or other unseemly methods or motives. Branches of the Church are left with theological holes and, missiologically, this bias misrepresents the Kingdom as condoning a culture of misogyny.

"Misogyny is a significant stumbling block to connecting with younger-generation people from post-Christendom cultures. The entire span of their formative years has been spent in the post-feminist era. They already have absorbed from a secular perspective a far deeper resonance with the radical realignment on gender that Bishop Wright speaks of as what happened during Jesus' ministry and the expansion of the early church. And that is stunning! Who could have predicted this? The tide of Western history is turning toward a pro-biblical stance on the parity of both genders as image-bearers, while at the same time it is turning away from institutionalized Christianity!

"What an opportunity to demonstrate Christ's radical perspective in words and deeds!

"Anyway, in my thoughts on the future, frankly, I am becoming more convinced that many of the misogynistic appearing denominations and movements will implode within 50 years. I'm not sure the syncretistic denominations and movements will last any longer. The traditional and pragmatic paradigms that segment and reduce complexity are in the midst of demise; holistic paradigms of paradox and balance are on the rise. So, I suspect those who theologically and ministerially split hairs should expect to find themselves in the dustbins of history. There's still time to correct our internal inconsistencies, though, and Bishop Wright leads in a most helpful direction."

Final thoughts for section one: theology creates culture and culture is a form of theology.

If the subtitle above is true, then we must act intentionally if we wish to include members of post-feminist generations in our churches and leave a legacy that they are willing to receive. We must push ourselves toward holistically resolving key issues in theology that create devastating, anti-biblical practices in our organizational culture. It is not the gospel that is causing offense, it is us. Our traditional branches (fundamental, conservative, evangelical, liberal, progressive) have paradigm problems, theological views, and organizational structures that complicate our ability to live into godly gender parity—and that apart from issues with church polity and women in ministry! If we refuse to resolve our hypocrisies with a biblically-based, holistic response, why should we expect our unholistic and unholy churches to survive?

Holistic paradigms, like the contemporary "missional movement," have a stronger opportunity to lead the Church to gender parity. Missional ministries match the cultural profile of these generations, with their focus on Kingdom-building, less hierarchical structure, and a producer mindset. Holistically-minded people are drawn to the missional focus of "being church" without the baggage of elaborate and exclusionary institutional structures of "doing church."

It's unfortunate that a Kingdom mentality finds itself at odds with the ways churches are run, but there it is. So, if conventional church leaders can't or won't resolve their paradigm issues, they should expect defection by next generation members from institutional churches toward missional/Kingdom enterprises. The Church will always increase, even if conventional-paradigm churches decrease.

Section two: What are better questions to ask?

New situations, new contexts, new questions

I recently read an intriguing account of personal and cultural change regarding gender relations. It came from a missionary friend working among former Muslims who now follow Jesus Christ. In the particular Islamic culture this group of disciples inherited, a husband is both permitted and expected to beat his wife for insubordination to the law or to him. The newly Christian men behaved in line with their background. They didn't know to behave differently until a local controversy arose from a public beating of an adolescent female for being alone in the presence of a man. Then some of these new disciples wondered how they should treat their wives now that they followed Jesus. They'd never asked such a question before, but their new allegiance raised new issues for them. As a result of studying teachings from the Bible, these men committed never to beat their wives again.

We men in post-Christendom cultures have some important things to learn from these former followers of Islam. They considered how to resist cultural expectations that contradict biblical requirements. They committed to change their personal actions to align with the Bible and thus became witnesses to transformation within their communities.

In the West, our starting point for resolving gender relationship issues is obviously far different from these brothers. But what exactly is it? What should we be asking? What cultural changes are raising new questions that challenge us to go to the Scriptures for fresh or refreshed responses? I'm not going to give all my best answers to these questions, so you readers can wrestle with these issues a while. But I will answer with how to create better questions.

Getting beyond conventional questions

First, I suggest we need to get beyond conventional questions regarding women and ministry—particularly about structures and roles in church polity. As we'll see in section three, we need to consider other core values. Polity is only part of the set or system, not the only thing or even the primary thing.

Second, the way we ask our questions preconditions the answers we receive. For instance, journalists are well known for their often irritating questions. These are frequently phrased in very negative terms, but that is in order to elicit a positive response. Other times, questions are worded more as a statement of the questioner's opinions than as a search for the interviewee's beliefs.

In gender relation issues, I've sometimes seen questions shut down a conversation by turning a dialogue into a debate, where one side volleys their Bible verses and the other side attempts a Scriptural scrimmage return. (Yes, I know I mixed my metaphors there, but 'twas on purpose. We just don't get very far along in the "game" when one side is playing tennis and the other side is playing football, do we?)

For instance, at an intergenerational forum in 2003, members of older generations and traditional paradigm churches were seeking to understand people from younger generations and holistic paradigm ministries. A pastor in his mid-60s asked the panel on which I sat, "I'm interested to know what you think about women as senior pastors." A few panelists took a stab at the theological and practical issues involved, and a few members of the audience then chimed in on this controversial issue. It got bogged down quickly. It felt like everyone was getting frustrated.

Finally, I raised my hand to be passed the microphone. I leaned forward and simply said, "I wasn't aware that the Bible commanded us to have senior pastors," and then sat back. There were a few moments of silence, and then some chuckles, and then some laughs. A bit more wrap-up by some other audience and panel members, and things moved on to a more productive topic.

That illustrates how a question that looked like a gender relations question may have had more to do with organizational system assumptions than about women in ministry. If a particular culture doesn't use the typical hierarchical pyramid of leadership and control, most women-in-ministry questions suddenly become irrelevant.

And guess what—from all I have observed, holistic paradigm cultures rarely have a stringent hierarchy for spiritual leadership. So, to them, a question about their leadership ladder makes no sense. (In fact, sometimes holistic paradigm cultures may be too flat in their authority structures, allowing young Christians to take roles of influence unsuitable for their maturity level, or toxic Christians to take control. But that just goes to show that every paradigm, and every culture that springs from it, has gaps and excesses.)

So, how do we begin to ask more relevant questions?

Section three: Why are we blocked from better questions?

The most relevant questions for the now-prominent holistic paradigm will come from our embracing their more comprehensive and integrated approach. They do have a biblical base, and adopting them will take time and intentionality for deep enough change to make a difference. Cosmetic changes to a flawed skin do not change flaws in the internal organs—health on the inside will show on the outside.

However, if this all seems too much too soon, at least we can attempt an intermediate step in the right direction, namely, to use a more comprehensive framework with which to consider gender relations. I suggest a fourfold theological framework:

Polarity—There are inherent differences between men and women. Besides obvious physiological differences, the brains of men and women are not configured quite the same, which creates differences in overall perception.

Complementarity—Those very differences are designed by God to be composited together for a greater good, because no one person has everything needed on their own to live out His plan. A couple, family, group, organization, church, or community needs both genders actively participating to create balance.

Parity—God values these differences equally, just as He equally values those who embody them.

Polity—This is the specific organizational structure of church, including how men and women fit with a church's or denomination's doctrine of spiritual gifts, general church leadership roles, and specific leadership roles/positions like deacon, elder, and pastor.

Most "discussions" about women in ministry over-focus on church polity. These often stall and get no farther than that. So, considering at least a combination of all four of these features is a step in the right direction toward normalizing gender relations. How do our differences actually help us have a fuller sense of God's working in our midst? How can we see these differences making us stronger, not strangers? Since God values us equally, what does that mean for how we should treat each other? Will "letting" women serve in areas they weren't allowed to before be a legitimate expression of a holistic viewpoint, or just another political move to supposedly level the playing field?

This sort of wider exploration can stretch our system toward a more comprehensive and holistic paradigm. And that is essential for developing an insider mentality into the paradigm and cultural systems that have bypassed the conventional modernist systems. Otherwise, we should fully expect women and men from a holistic paradigm either to avoid us for our apparent hypocrisy, or to call us to account for appearances of gender inequity practices that conflict with their beliefs or invalidate what we say we believe.

Section four: What happens if we integrate a holistic paradigm?

As I stated at the beginning, I believe we need to consider the overall context of our approach before we jump into the content of our actions. So, what would it look like if we were to reorient our approach around a more holistic paradigm? Let me leave you with a metaphor instead of a list.

My friends Joshua and Kristen recently saw the entire extended editions of the Lord of the Rings trilogy for the first time. They remembered the much shorter theatrical versions from years before, and how the focus seemed centered around Frodo and the ring. They were stunned at how the addition of two hours of whole scenes and added-in bits changed the focus to Aragorn becoming the King. The plots involving Frodo and the Hobbits didn't disappear, but, amazingly, there was an astonishing new picture that emerged as Aragorn gradually accepted his identity and destiny, identified with humanity, and was willing to sacrifice all for the sake of his people.

When missing material that the director intended is integrated back into a film, the themes of the story change because we see character and plot development as it was always meant to be. When we expand our paradigm and embrace a larger framework for gender relations in church, we will experience church in the larger ways God always intended—a "Director's Cut" edition of being church, if you will. From my 35 years of experience in learning to be an agent of healing in broken gender relations, I am convinced the "extended edition" is worth the time.

Other resources

"Helen Haste Quote on Generations and Measuring Change," blog post by Brad Sargent, October 25, 2009: http://futuristguy.wordpress.com/2009/10/25/helen-haste-quote-on-generations-and-measuring-change/

"Paradigm Transition: Do we have just 25 years to do this?" blog post by Brad Sargent, June 28, 2009: http://futuristguy.wordpress.com/2008/06/28/paradigm-transition-do-we-have-just-25-years-to-do-this/

Brad Sargent is a culturologist, futurist, and organizational systems developer. He has a 35-plus year record as a practitioner and theoretician in promoting the providentially equal value of both genders. In his younger years he sampled theological and political forms of fundamentalism, conservatism, evangelicalism, liberalism, and progressivism. Dissatisfied with the deficits and excesses he experienced in each, he eventually moved toward a more comprehensive and holistic re-integration of his faith. However, one element that continued through those searching years and beyond was a commitment to take people at face value (which he learned from family members who are what the Bible terms "people of peace"), regardless of unchangeable characteristics as gender, age, race, or abilities. He blogs at http://futuristguy.wordpress.com.

Wikiklesia Volume 2 Taking Flight
Why We Need Mothers & Fathers, Sisters & Brothers, Daughters & Sons
Kathy Escobar

From near the beginning, we have wrestled with the broken parts of our humanity which have undermined our freedom and wholeness. With God's image in us broken, our capacity for deep and intimate relationship is diminished. A huge piece of the Christian story has to do with Jesus restoring us back to wholeness, his reminding us of "who we really are" in Christ, and his renewing our ability to love and be loved. And while it is easy to talk about this individually, the truth is that collectively the beautiful and wild Body of Christ is damaged and in desperate need of the type of restoration that requires far more love in deed than in words.

So many *know* that the Body of Christ needs restoration, healing, and transformation when it comes to issues of gender. We desire it deeply. The bigger question is *how do we change?* How can we participate tangibly, actively, and practically in the healing of "the church?" How can we break down the walls that divide genders and keep us cut off from freedom, hope, and peace? How can we learn what it really means to live alongside each other in true and powerful community together?

I think that the purpose of community—"the church"—is to be a place where people can both learn to love God and others as well as to be loved by God and others. Like so many things that matter, this does not magically drop out of the sky. It comes through hard work, investment in relationship, and openness to the movement of the Spirit of God in us and through us. And these relationships with God and people are all tangled up together; too often we try to compartmentalize these relationships and deal with them separately. But, this seems contrary to the message of Love in the scriptures.

Jesus summed up the law—love God, love your neighbors as yourselves—in Mark 12, which is the essence of our Christian journey. I often say *"You can't love God without loving your neighbors, you can't love your neighbors without loving God, and it's hard to love either one when we don't love ourselves."*

I have been in ministry for over 15 years, and over the course of that time I have taken a lot of flak for over-promoting "healing" in the church. Many churches are known for their programs, preaching, and music, but little else. I am not saying those things are bad, but the role of "the church" was never to be about form, but rather teaching and modeling the ways of Christ's love. I'm guessing that resistance to "healing and recovery" stems mainly from fear. *Healing means we will have to humbly look at what's missing, what's broken, what's hurting, what's wounded, what is in desperate need of transformation.* For me, the word "healing" is synonymous with "spiritual transformation." *Our formation into the image of Christ means becoming more whole in our ability to love God, our neighbors, and ourselves.*

Christians often forget what an important role each of us plays in the spiritual formation of another. There are so many different aspects to God's character that one person here on earth of course can't reflect them all. But the sum of diverse, powerful, and healing relationships through true community can transform people and magnify God's image in amazing ways. This is why incarnational, redemptive community *across genders* is critically important. Men and women need each other. Men don't just need men and women don't just need women because, though we are individually broken, together we reflect the full image of God.

We all have a story of brokenness, no matter how big or small. Some of that is rooted in our family of origin; some in different life experiences. For instance, I am an adult child of an alcoholic. If you look at a here's-what-adult-children-of-an-alcoholic-might-be-like list, I personify almost every characteristic: I have always wanted a dad who was present, who would fight for me, protect me, and cheer me on. My biological dad couldn't do the things I longed and wished for. But in the past five-and-a-half years, I have experienced redemptive healing in incredible ways as I have entered into a deep and transforming relationship with my friend Mike, and he has experienced the same with me. We always joke that I am his mother, daughter, sister, friend, and teammate, and that he is my father, son, brother, friend, and teammate— all at once in some mysterious way. Part of my soul has been restored through this relationship and I am much freer because of it. Because of this relationship I can now stand on more solid ground—I'm more whole. If we had been intimidated about entering each other's lives, we would have missed so much of God's heart for both of us.

I strongly believe that the segregation of men and women from each other in our church practices is damaging and does not reflect the Kingdom of God. Men and women serving side-by-side in the trenches of real life together—learning, healing, and growing—is necessary for true redemptive community. Opportunities for transformation will not be available if we keep each other at arm's length.

Often, people believe wholeheartedly that women should have an equal and important voice in "the church" yet they continue to perpetuate a system that doesn't allow it to happen. Within our thinking is entrenched an odd and sad disconnect between theory and practice, rhetoric and reality. For real change and healing to occur, we must practice what we preach. As leaders, we must boldly and humbly explore our weaknesses in the area of male-female relationships, willingly examining our hearts and practices before we expect others to dive in.

Here are a few ways to begin to live some of this out in tangible ways:

Women and men must have an equal voice.

This means that we hear from both genders, not just once in a while, but as a natural rhythm of life together. Those with the microphone have an incredible amount of influence and power. When the microphone (leadership) is held by both men and women equally, something very powerful and healing happens. It reduces fear. The divide between us diminishes. We start to realize how much we can learn from each other. When we hear from the typically "missing half" of the population, we start to realize we can't live without it. I can't say how deeply saddened I am that Jesus-followers have intentionally limited the voice of women. The wisdom that is missed is a deep loss.

We can devote ourselves to creating spaces where men and women share freely.

At the church I helped found, The Refuge, we do not just talk about this—we do it. Women and men together often facilitate our gatherings, no matter how big or small. Sometimes the lead is a woman, sometimes it's a man. Almost always we hear from both. For us it seems natural, yet this didn't happen without a lot of work by everyone. Sometimes men have had to step aside and women have had to step up. For me, stepping up was easier said than done. When we first planted The Refuge, I needed some pushing. I needed my friends to say, "We want your voice." I needed my partners to say, "Go for it." I needed God to settle down some of the crazy voices in my head that said, "You can't, you shouldn't." I have since learned that a big part of my role is to pass the microphone to others. To push, to pull, to make more room for a diversity of voices that crosses far more barriers than gender. It takes work to equalize voices, but I believe it is a critical piece of healing "the church" needs, and it is worth every bit of energy it requires.

We must cultivate real relationships with each other, and this requires intention, time, and risk.

I do not believe "going to" church will do the trick, nor do I think there's some kind of program that can make these kinds of relationships possible. It will mean boldly practicing being together—men and women in the same room, around the same table, sharing our stories, our fears, dreams, hurts, hopes, and generally spending time together beyond just the periphery. It means engaging in conflict, weeping together, celebrating together, and nurturing an interdependence that is sometimes foreign for many of us (especially in a world and culture that espouses independence, control, and selfishness).

I am grateful to live in a community that is intentionally trying to live out these values. It means that we don't segregate men and women, even when some of the conversation centers on deep issues of the heart. The church can glean from Alcoholics Anonymous in many ways. On the whole, AA is a mixed group. Most issues aren't women's or men's issues—they are human issues. Listening to, learning from, and challenging each other requires us sitting side by side, not just once in a while, but consistently over a long period of time. Sometimes people say things that are hard to hear, but in reality far more healing happens than meets the eye.

We have to learn to take sexual awkwardness out of the picture, and this will take practice.

We live in a world saturated with unaddressed sexual brokenness and exploitation, so much so that this concept may be the most difficult to navigate. I believe one of the reasons there is so much sexual brokenness today is that we have not learned how to be together as mothers and fathers, brothers and sisters, as equals, with a purity of heart and spirit. The onus doesn't just fall on men—women too have received and played out the subtle and direct messages that say *"men and women can never be just friends."* Fear always divides and alienates us; it never leads us toward reconciliation.

True restoration and reconciliation means learning to become more comfortable with each other as friends, recovering the lost heart of brotherly-sisterly love. One of the reasons I am passionate about co-pastoring with a man is that it is a way to live this out, refusing to re-create the imbalanced power dynamics that too often exist in church leadership. I have a lot of brothers. We meet for coffee or we call each other when we need fresh perspective. We challenge and encourage each other in love. We fight. It is real. It is pure. It is healing. Early in life I was taught how to use my sexuality to either get what I needed or to fill an emotional void that needed filling. Much damage was done to myself and others. Now, I am learning how to have healthy relationships with men other than my husband, all of which have strengthened me.

Start to notice places in our own hearts, story, and spiritual experiences that need noticing.

What do we long for? Or, the flip side of that question, what is God trying to reveal to us that we may not want to look at? Answering these questions requires a quietness, an inner searching, humility. It also requires the discipline of not thinking about other people and what they need, but focusing on our own journey, our own hearts. I have a gut reflex all the time that says, *"I don't want to need anyone! I can't need anyone!"* I know I am not the only one with a spirit of self-reliance that shuts down intimate relationships with others and God. But, becoming more honest about our own personal barriers to relationship is an important and necessary piece of moving toward restoration and healing across genders.

Humility

We are often disconnected from how self-reliant we might really be. We are affirmed and trained to believe our independence and strength is critical to our abilities. Many of us have been taught through our Christian experiences to ignore or neglect our brokenness and pretend that things are better than they really are. Noticing our own personal inabilities and wounds requires a great deal of humility, self-reflection, and courage. My recognition that it is only when I am humble, open, and honest about my weaknesses that I receive healing and hope was a significant step for me. I found that the more I pretended, the lonelier I felt. *Needing others* doesn't come naturally, and I often have to force myself to share, to let others in, and to accept that despite my strengths I am terribly weak and needy.

Rely on others to fill in the gaps and respect our own limitations.

None of us alone can fill the huge and blaring gaps in others' experiences. The healthy approach involves bringing whatever we can to the relationship and letting God do the rest. It's important that we don't think the burden is all on us, but as leaders, innovators, and community cultivators we can intentionally create a culture where others feel encouraged to step in to each other's lives in small and meaningful ways. This is why diversity in community is so important—we need all kinds of voices, roles, perspectives, differences. We can use our influence and discernment to draw as many people as we can into the mix.

We do this at The Refuge by intentionally creating support teams that include both men and women. There is a strange tension in developing healthy cross-gender relationships between needing others and making sure we don't demand or expect more from one another than is realistic. Real change takes time, and we must remember to trust the larger story and not focus on the minutia. Often we will feel discouraged, exposed, tired, and plain old irritated by how difficult it is to live in true brother-sister community with each other.

We need guides to inspire and teach us.

The idea of mothers and fathers, sisters and brothers, and daughters and sons in the Body of Christ is not common, and models are in short supply. It's not for lack of desire, it's for lack of skill and not knowing where to start. I believe it is critical that those who have experienced this dynamic to help others on the journey. For me, this included intentionally pursuing relationships with two other communities who were dedicated to co-pastoring and gender equality. Exposing myself to practitioners in the trenches helped me fan into flame some of my dreams for our community. I asked questions. I listened. I soaked in what I could. It started with an intentional pursuit of a relationship with a guide or mentor. Now, after being associated with these more experienced practitioners for the past three years, the learning is going both ways. I am positive we would not be where we are as a community without this exchange of information, and I am positive I would not be where I am as a person or as a leader without this collaboration.

It is important to note that there is no perfect formula. Part of maturing spiritually and leading well requires listening to God and to others to discern direction. Sometimes the things that we try will fail miserably. Sometimes an idea that worked well for one community or group is not appropriate for another. The key is finessing what we learn from our mentors and being willing to experiment and adjust along the way.

While I passionately believe that this is all possible, I also want to respect that as we move toward learning the skills of brotherly and sisterly love, it is important to not be naive. We are human and there are things that can go terribly wrong without a lot of strength, intention, and God's spirit at work in us. Here are some things we can keep in mind:

Keep relationships out in the open.

Cross-gender friendships work if nothing is hidden. The relationships are formed in community, open to others. While I am not personally apprehensive about one-on-one interactions, I believe a fuller and richer experience of meeting with three or more people instead of two can provide additional emotional safety.

Intention is required, especially among people who haven't practiced this before.

We have friends in our community who have said, *"I need to learn how to be just friends with women (or men). Help me."* We help by facilitating conversations about what we need from each other, how to communicate honestly, and how to resolve anything that doesn't feel safe. This helps build a solid foundation for healthy relationships. My role as a pastor is to help create spaces for this to happen.

Listen carefully to warnings we might have.

It is a big responsibility to live together in true Christian community, men and women side-by-side. We must be humble enough to listen for not only God's voice and that of wise friends, but also the voice inside of us that might be warning that something isn't right. When we listen well and are willing to share what we're hearing with others, we can obtain wise input to navigate to a healthier place when necessary.

Living out these values and principles are challenging and not for the faint-hearted. Those committed to this kind of walk are not choosing the path of least resistance. However, none of the Kingdom principles are easy. Almost everything Jesus calls us to is counter-cultural, odd, uncomfortable, hard, and often perceived as heretical. There are many who disagree that this kind of side-by-side community is possible. They've built upon techniques and procedures or a few passages of scripture and called it a day. I believe *that* is taking the easy way out and is utterly inconsistent with the kind of crossing-all-the-boundaries-of-this-world example that Christ gives us in the gospels. The question is, are we brave enough to follow his ways rather than those of a particular system that has been impressed upon us? Many are sensing that the approaches we've had in the past are no longer effective. We need restoration. We need healing. We need each other.

Healthy, healing, transforming relationships across gender are missing in the body of Christ. Fear and lack of good models obstruct change. Many leaders have adopted the methods of the world and forgotten the example of early church mothers and fathers. It's time to revisit our roots—messy, organic, intense, healing community was the norm. The family of God grew up together and spread the love they experienced to the world.

Let's listen to what God is stirring up in us as leaders, as cultivators of innovation and healing. We serve in a broken, hurting world that needs God and the transformational relationships that result from knowing Him. And may we be brave enough to be mothers, fathers, brothers, sisters, daughters, and sons to each other, a beautiful reflection of God's wholeness lived out together.

Kathy Escobar is a co-pastor at The Refuge, an eclectic faith community in Denver, CO. She is a trained spiritual director, a group facilitator, and an advocate for friends in hard places. Kathy is a cultivator of Voca Femina, a creative arts site for women to use their voice. Kathy conducts workshops at various conferences and is also an online faculty instructor. As a writer, she has written various articles on Biblical equality, the stained glass ceiling, and being a suburban missional. Kathy has co-authored

Why We Need Mothers & Fathers... Kathy Escobar

Come with Me: An Invitation to Break Through the Walls Between You and God *and* Refresh: Sharing Stories, Building Faith. *Kathy writes for "Communitas Collective", "Voca Femina," and blogs at "The Carnival in My Head" and "The Refuge." Kathy is a mom of 5 (3 teenagers & twins), teammate and partner of 19 years with her husband, and readily admits, "My life is wonderfully crazy and full, chaotic and fun."*

"Remember no one can make you feel inferior without your consent." —— Eleanor Roosevelt

"The most common way people give up their power is by thinking they don't have any." ——Alice Walker

Wikiklesia Volume 2 Taking Flight
Coloring Outside the Christian Circle
Becky Garrison

Those theological thinkers throughout history who have relegated Mary Magdalene to the role of "prostitute" have bitten more off the apple than they can chew. These post-Constantinian empire builders seems to have conveniently forgotten that she was the very first person to witness the Risen Christ (Mark 16:1-8, Matthew 28:1-10, Luke 22:55-24:1-11, John 20:1-18). Then again, even the disciples dismissed the women's firsthand accounts as nonsense, thus demonstrating the lack of respect accorded to women in first century Judea (Luke 24:11).

But throughout his ministry Jesus overturned this notion that women held the same status as the family donkey by embracing women as equals in the Kingdom of God. After he hung out a bit with a Samaritan woman at a public well, his unclean acts made the front page of *The Pharisee Post* (John 4:4-26). He showed mercy to a woman about to be stoned for adultery (John 8:1-12). Despite his disciples' objections, he embraced a female sinner who crashed a dinner party because she wanted to anoint his feet with oil (Luke 7:36-50). As much as Jesus appreciated Martha's cooking, he invited Mary to join the all-boys theological discussion instead of washing dishes (Luke 10:38-42).

When a crowd said to Jesus that his mother and brother were looking for him, Jesus looked at those sitting in a circle around him and responded, "Here are my mother and my brothers!" (Mark 3:31-35). According to Jewish customs of the time, Jesus would not have said "mother and brothers" had there not been female disciples gathered around him.

Citations of women like Lydia, Phoebe, Prisca (Priscilla), and Chloe bolster the claim that women played pivotal roles in those churches formed after Pentecost (see Acts 16:40; Romans 16:1-16, and 1 Corinthians 1:11). Even after Constantine converted, one can still find accounts of figures such as St. Brigid of Kildare (approximately 453-525 CE),[1] who by all accounts was one major holy hiney-kicker. Over time, she wielded considerable influence over the Church of Ireland, even appointing her own bishops.

In *The Future of Faith*, theologian Harvey Cox describes a ninth-century mosaic in the Church of St. Praxedia in Rome depicting St. Theodora with the word *episcopa* ("bishop") inscribed above her head. Here, within walking distance to the main train station in Rome, one can find an icon that represents one of the hottest skirmishes in current historical research and received practices and traditions. Simply put, what did the term *episcopa* mean in Theodora's day? Was she the convener or president of a local congregation? Or did she have a wider responsibility? Was she "ordained," and if so, what did ordination mean then? How does this mosaic fit in with pictures of women leading what appear to be Eucharistic services like the *Fractio Panis* ("Breaking the Bread") found in Catacombs of Priscilla?[2]

Fast forward, oh, some two thousand years, give or take a few decades, and yes, in some denominations one can find women in some

---

[1] http://www.solasbhride.ie
[2] See *The Future of Faith*, page 180-181

key leadership positions, especially in Pentecostal circles. In fact, I come from a tradition where currently a woman gets to wear the biggest pointy hat. So, one might think that "we've come a long way, baby" and are truly seen as equal prayer partners.

But as the saying goes, history is written by the winners, and those in charge tend to put themselves in the front and center of the story. A quick trip through Amazon.com will demonstrate that except for Christian fiction, children's books and material geared towards the Suitable Helper and True Women® market, the bulk of material churned out for the Christian market remains male-dominated. Thanks to the cookbooks churned out by some of these authors, one can learn how to create a church that is

Deep/Devotional/Dogma-free
Emergent/Entertainment/Engagement
Holy/Homey/Heretical
Missional/Messy/Magical
Pastoral/Prophetic/Post-evangelical
Real/Re-imagined/Religionless

In these books, these mostly male Martha Stewarts of the church world whip up a dish that looks camera ready and wows the audience. Martha and these missional males want us to think they're just like the rest of us, and therein lies the rub. They both spend so much time on stage that they seldom eat at home. Hence, they tend to present an idealized representation of their world which often doesn't depict the real deal. And like Martha, they attract their share of female groupies who worship them as icons. Even when one puts on an event that's more gender inclusive, just follow the money and all too often it's clear that the men are the ones in charge of the overall production.

But if one chooses to venture off the center stage, one can find hordes of people living out what it means to be the church of the 21st century. I remember when I was covering HipHopEmass in the Bronx,[3] I overlooked Jeannine Otis at first, even though she helped craft the first setting of the Episcopal Eucharist to hip-hop.

Rather than marketing herself as a holy hip-hop artist, she put her focus on creating a communal vibe where all could rap for the glory of God. Hence, she wasn't concerned about safeguarding her street cred. Had her story not been told in my book *Rising from the Ashes: Rethinking Church* she would have faded into the background as yet another woman whose spiritual story got erased from the history books.

Other places I have found signs of God kicking spiritual butt include Church of the Apostles, based in the funky Freemont Section of Seattle,[4] and the radically welcoming Boston-based The Crossing.[5] Often those working on the margins tend to be women or ethnic minorities who choose not to enter into the church power games, preferring instead to find their own place to play. As the Rev. Stephanie Spellers of The Crossing explained to me, "I don't have any illusion that I'll be made bishop." The Rev. Karen Ward, Abbess of Church of the Apostles, echoes this sentiment, adding that she brings trouble to the Episcopal Church. However, she doesn't see "trouble" as a bad thing because, after all, God troubled the waters at creation.

In their own ways, these women create a synergy that emits sparks which others within their respective communities use to build

---

[3] http://www.episcopalchurch.org/26769_48886_ENG_HTM.htm

[4] http://www.youtube.com/watch?v=YPJHYRAuDNw

[5] http://www.youtube.com/watch?v=NA53Z-JKfjc

their own faith fires. Before you know it, a bonfire has been born that's far more magnificent than if they had kept the focus shining on them.

Also, these three women, who coincidentally happen to be African American, blow apart the misguided myth propagated by a few post-evangelical males that the institutional church is DOA. In a proposal entitled "Seize the Episcopal Moment: An Emergent Manifesto of Hope for the Episcopal Church,"[6] the Rev. Karen Ward and the Rev. Donald Schell, one of the founders of St. Gregory of Nyssa in San Francisco, offer some helpful signposts that can move the conversation of emerging mission forward in the Episcopal Church. As long as the church contains beacons of hope like Jeannine, Karen, and Stephanie, then glimpses of God can still shine through.

Missiologist and blogger Andrew Jones[7] predicts women, such as missional entrepreneur Shannon Hopkins[8], will be leading the charge in terms of spearheading grassroots social justice endeavors. As he notes, "Emerging church energies will be re-directed from creative worship arts to creative social enterprises which will enable long term sustainability."

So, when people complain they can't find any women in ministry, I tell them that perhaps they've been looking for love in all the wrong places. Practitioners who build truly transformative communities tend to focus on the work at hand instead of pimping themselves on the author/speaker circuit. While they might get some press coverage for their ministries, they don't seek the glare of the media spotlight. They

---

6 http://anglimergent.ning.com/profiles/blogs/seize-the-episcopal-moment-an

7 http://tallskinnykiwi.typepad.com/

8 http://www.sweetnotions.org

know that by giving up one's personal power, the power of the Holy Spirit can spread like wildfire. Such is the paradox of power.

Then again, God's full of upside-down surprises throughout the Bible. As authors and activists Shane Claiborne and Chris Haw pointed out during their *Jesus for President: Politics for Ordinary Radicals* tour, "Consider the paradox and humor of God's audacious power: a stuttering prophet will become the voice of God, a barren old lady will become the mother of a nation, a shepherd boy will become their king, and a homeless boy will lead them home." To that I would add, "The Risen Christ chose to reveal himself to a person who was deemed property and redeemed her to be equal in his eyes." Therein lies the power of the Gospel when seen through the eyes of the risen Christ.

Becky Garrison is a Contributing Editor for "Sojourners" and a blogger with the "God's Politics" blog. Her books include Jesus Died for This?: A Satirist's Search for the Risen Christ *(Zondervan, August 2010),* The New Atheist Crusaders and their Unholy Grail *(Thomas Nelson, 2007),* Rising from the Ashes: Rethinking Church *(Seabury Books, 2007), and* Red and Blue God: Black and Blue Church *(Jossey Bass, 2006). Additional writing credits include work for "The High Calling," "Killing the Buddha," "Geez," "US Catholic" and "The Wittenburg Door." Presently she is working on another book for Zondervan and a two book series exploring new forms of UK-US Anglican church for Church Publishing. Follow her travels on Twitter, @JesusDied4This, and on her website, www.beckygarrison.com.*

Bill Gates recalls once being invited to speak in Saudi Arabia, finding himself facing a segregated audience. Four-fifths of the listeners were men, on the left. The remaining one-fifth were women, all covered in black cloaks and veils, on the right. A partition separated the two groups. Toward the end, in the question-and-answer session, a member of the audience noted that Saudi Arabia aimed to be one of the top 10 countries in the world in technology by 2010 and asked if that was realistic. "Well, if you're not fully utilizing half the talent in the country," Gates said, "you're not going to get too close to the Top 10." The small group on the right erupted in wild cheering.

Wikiklesia Volume 2 Taking Flight
Women Hold the Keys to a Sustainable Future
Anna Clark

"Things are getting worse, things are getting better, and things are already perfect." When professors Sean Esbjorn-Hargens and Michael Zimmerman coined this phrase, they were speaking about ecology, but these words could just as easily describe the state of the women's movement. However, the environmental movement and the women's movement are particularly intertwined in that they belong to the same era and share the same fundamental goal: to foster a fairer, more just society. So how is it that these movements are increasingly at odds with each other?

Speaking as a working mother—in the sustainability field, no less—I recognize the irony of this statement. I admit that I love to work. I like being engaged in the world, making a difference, and of course, making money. But I also know that enjoying these benefits makes me privileged. For many more women, a dual-income society demands they hold down one, even two, unfulfilling jobs just to pay the rent. Paradoxically, as we work harder to improve our quality of life, we have less time for the stuff of life: community, family, friendships, and even good food. Fast food, which now feeds a quarter of the country on any given day, is contributing to a startling epidemic in obesity and waste. It's little wonder that Americans, who represent five percent of the earth's population, use 30 percent of its resources.

Women Hold the Keys to a Sustainable Future Anna Clark

The harsh underbelly of our success in the workplace is that it feeds the same economic engine that causes inflation, burns energy, and squanders natural resources. We may be making more money, but we spend more on childcare, groceries, and just about everything else. We experience more success, but we endure more stress. Consequently, some of our hard-won independence is illusory.

While there is no single solution to this quandary, there is so much we can do as individuals that we aren't yet doing. Sustainability—defined as "meeting the needs of the present without compromising the needs of the future"—is loaded with practical benefits. Green living helps us save money, get healthy, and protect our future. It can even be an expression of our faith and a way to serve God. Given women's natural inclination for building communities and helping others, environmental stewardship represents a virtually untapped opportunity for us to lead in the 21st century.

As the women's movement continues to unfurl, we need to confront the unpleasant, if unintended and largely hidden, consequences of our progress if we want to forge a sustainable future for everyone else. The dire condition of our natural world and its people demands that we act in order to protect God's creation. Unless and until we do, we will continue contributing to the very problems we claim we want to solve.

***

The standard of living has improved a great deal for women in the past century, and this is a very good thing. Consider the lifestyle of your typical early 20th century female worker, the shirtwaist maker. The shirtwaist, an all-occasion blouse worn with an ankle-length skirt, freed women from the uncomfortable constraint of corsets. Thanks to a steady stream of immigrant workers, the booming ready-to-wear clothing industry made the stylish shirtwaist affordable to almost everyone. A typical shirtwaist maker, as young as age 15, worked twelve hours a day, seven days a week, and typically earned about $6 per week. She was often required to use her own needles, thread, irons, and occasionally her own sewing machine. A young worker described one factory as "unsanitary—that's the word that is generally used, but there ought to be a worse one used."[1]

As undesirable as the life of a shirtwaist maker was, it pales in comparison to the death of one. On March 25, 1911, 146 such workers, mostly teenage girls, perished in a fire at the headquarters of the Triangle Shirtwaist Factory. Within ten minutes, the entire ninth floor was ablaze as flames leapt from workstation to workstation. Many died while jumping to their deaths from the roof of the ten-story Asch Building. Only a few survivors managed to flee the fire, for the doors to the fire escapes were locked. At the Triangle factory, women had to leave the building to use the bathroom, so management began locking the steel exit doors to prevent the "interruption of work." Rescue workers found skeletons leaning over sewing machines and melted bodies huddled against doors. Public outrage over the cruel treatment and senseless deaths of so many girls contributed to legislation that would protect American workers from such atrocities.

---

1 http://www.aflcio.org/aboutus/history/history/uprising_fire.cfm

Women Hold the Keys to a Sustainable Future   Anna Clark

For the better part of the twentieth century, the garment district thrived, offering employment, freedom, and entrée to the middle class for thousands of immigrant workers, both male and female. This was capitalism at its finest. But in any political scheme or economic system, idealism morphs into pragmatism every time. Those in positions of power will justify self-serving policies. People a few notches down will learn to strive within the system rather combat it, lest they miss a chance to improve their station. People at the bottom are helplessly stuck. This phenomenon was blatant in 1960s Communist China, but in America in 2010, injustice is more subtle, hidden from sight and certainly out of mind.

Today, the nearly vacant garment district, which made 95 percent of our clothing in 1965 but now makes only 5 percent, reflects the state of manufacturing in America. Yesterday's Seventh Avenue shirtwaist workers are today's third-world factory workers. The garment industry, Bangladesh's largest income earner, employs more than 2 million workers (mostly women), bringing the impoverished nation $11 billion annually.[2] But the destitute women who make our cheap clothes today labor under conditions very similar to those of American workers a century ago. Here's a case in point: In 2000, 91 years after the Triangle Shirtwaist fire, over 100 workers lost their lives in a fire in the KTS Textile Industries Ltd. Factory, a sweatshop in Bangladesh. The main emergency exit was illegally locked. Many of the dead and missing were 12, 13, 14 and 15 year-old girls who were paid just seven cents an hour. Bodies were burnt beyond recognition.[3]

---

2 http://boston.indymedia.org/feature/display/208130

3 http://www.nlcnet.org/article.php?id=112

Despite these tragedies, women do have more opportunities than ever before. So how do we balance the great with the not so good? As an American woman of the professional class, I have all the freedom and resources that my third-world sisters do not. But lately, I've found myself wondering what "success" really means. Sure I've got the money to spend, at least relatively speaking, but do I really need to buy all this stuff? How can I use my position and resources to help others who are less fortunate? What behaviors should I model to help my children lead in the future? Am I the only one asking these questions?

***

American pop culture's portrayal of the "ideal woman" undergoes a dramatic shift at least once a generation. One of our most enduring cultural icons is Rosie the Riveter, the muscle-flexing World War II-era dame who inspired women to leave their kitchens to work in the munitions factories. Even more riveting was Alice Paul, the real-life crusader for woman's suffrage, recently portrayed by Hilary Swank in HBO's recent film *Iron Jawed Angels*. Thanks to Alice Paul's efforts—which earned her prison and torture, and us the 18th Amendment—women can vote, own property, earn college degrees, compete in the professional world, and hold office.

One hundred years later we are doing so well for ourselves that we are beginning to pass up the guys. Almost all income growth in the U.S. over the past two decades has come from women, while men have seen flat or declining incomes. By around 2028, the average woman is projected to earn more than the average man in the U.S.[4] Over the next five years, the global incomes of women are estimated to grow from

---

4 http://blog.nielsen.com/nielsenwire/global/below-the-topline-womens-growing-economic-power/

$13 trillion to $18 trillion. That incremental $5 trillion is nearly twice the growth in GDP expected from China and India combined. Globally, women are the biggest emerging market ever seen.[5]

Marketing executives are turning this to their advantage. Here is one marketing consultant's assessment of women's untapped "potential":

> "We are continuously doing research on "why she buys" to give us insight into the impact that female consumers have on the marketplace. Much of what we learn in school is based on the age-old rules that were established when men ran the show. Not so much anymore.
>
> Check out these five global trends and take note:
>
> 1. The presence of more women in the workforce changes everything. Women are on the go and convenience is the name of the game.
>
> 2. Delayed marriage means more money spent on me. Luxury goods, apparel and cosmetics are the only industries really to take note of a single woman's power to purchase. When will everyone else catch up?

---

[5] Ibid.

3. Lower birthrates globally mean few kids, but more stuff. Kids today own more stuff than ever before. Luxuries of yesterday have now become passé.

4. The divorce economy means two of everything. Smaller households create the need to have your own.

5. The presence of older women redefines target market. Gone are the days of gold lamé and shuffleboard tournaments. Today's older person adapts to technology and has powerful market influence."[6]

***

If you haven't heard of affluenza, be warned. It began with the post-World War II boom, but a more dangerous strain of this virus appeared in America sometime during the 1980s. Waning only briefly during the height of the recession, the epidemic continues to loom as a threat. In fact, it's now spreading full tilt to India and China.

aff•lu•en•za, n. 1. The bloated, sluggish and unfulfilled feeling that results from efforts to keep up with the Joneses. 2. An epidemic of stress, overwork, waste and indebtedness caused by the pursuit of the American Dream. 3. An unsustainable addiction to economic growth.

---

[6] http://bakercreative.wordpress.com/2009/08/21/insight-into-the-power-of-women-spending-in-the-global-marketplace/

Most of us don't recognize affluenza in ourselves because yesterday's luxuries have become today's necessities. We can no longer differentiate needs versus wants.

With so much emphasis on the material, it's no wonder that one of today's most prominent stereotypes is the "soccer mom." One South Carolina paper defines her as:

> "A well-heeled super-parent whose primary mission in life is to do too much for her children. She got on a waiting list early for the right day-care center, sent junior to Montessori, started violin lessons at five, private school the same year, and the next year—soccer."[7]

UrbanDictionary.com offers another definition that pretty well sums up most folks' impressions of the soccer mom, describing her as:

> "A woman who refuses to believe that anything that is not white Christian middle-upper class is evil. Political correctness and purification of youth is the prime goal of this group. These 'dress and act like we are 20 even though we all know we are double that age' sufferers are often found destroying the sacred environment in their oversized SUV's driving in an unsafe fashion, often times with cell phones in one hand and a Starbucks coffee in the other."[8]

---

[7] http://www.slate.com/id/2255/
[8] http://www.urbandictionary.com/define.php?term=soccer%20mom&page=2

The soccer mom has become such a fixture in American culture that presidential campaigns now cater to this growing demographic.

I recognize that I'm painting with broad strokes here, but we dismiss pop-cultural characterizations, TV characters, and advertising images as powerless at our own risk. In a culture where people of average means have the resources to satisfy their whims, life does, in fact, imitate art. Shows like *Sex and the City*, *Desperate Housewives*, and the gamut of reality TV programs demonstrate how "success," as popularly defined, is beginning to fray at the edges. The new strong female archetype shows up like the über-independent, oft-divorced career woman dripping in designer clothes, dining out every night, and desperately clinging to her youth. Even if these are not my values or your values per se, these values have seized our culture through the media. This reality is being reflected back at us through our children.

According to a recent in-depth study in England, the lack of cohesion and family life are creating a wave of "anti-social behavior, materialism and the cult of celebrity." The study also states, "Today's children, it was generally felt, are being forced to grow up too soon and the prospects for society and the world they will inhabit look increasingly perilous." The comprehensive study, which brings in perspectives from teachers, also reports widespread dissatisfaction with the standards of modern parenting. It complains of parents' low aspirations for children and said many were "passing the buck for their children's socialization to schools." The authors of the study said the cumulative evidence had shown "deep anxiety about the condition of childhood today and the society and world in which children are growing up."[9]

***

---

[9] http://www.independent.co.uk/news/education/education-news/the-primary-cause-for-concern-396669.html

Not being a sociologist, I can't trace the precise point in time where women's rights went wrong. Absent a more academic analysis, I would say that we simply grew apathetic. For some, success breeds complacency. For many others, just trying to make a living occupies every waking moment. People who don't have control over their own lives don't usually feel equipped to change the system. They are just too focused on surviving.

Those of us who do enjoy life on the higher rungs of the ladder can help turn the tide by making new decisions. For starters, we can wield our power in the marketplace. Here are the latest figures:

- Women globally will control $18 trillion in annual consumer spending by 2014.[10]

- Women presently control or substantially influence 65% of the world's annual consumer spending. For items such as clothing, food, and expenses for the children, women control upwards of 85% of the spending.[11]

- Women own more than 47% of the stocks.[12]

- Women-owned firms (50% or more) account for 40% of all privately held firms, employing more than 13 million people.[13]

---

10 http://edition.cnn.com/2009/WORLD/asiapcf/10/25/intl.women.global.economy/

11 http://blog.nielsen.com/nielsenwire/global/below-the-topline-womens-growing-economic-power/

12 http://stopharass.com/article-women-marketplace.htm

13 http://www.womensbusinessresearchcenter.org/research/keyfacts/

With so much economic power, what a difference we could make if we would:

- Lean on corporations to create more opportunities to work from home, which saves money for families, reduces our environmental burden on society, and lowers the energy load in office buildings. It also helps free America from its dependency on petroleum, which fuels 97 percent of our transportation sector.

- Buy greener products. Labels such as "fair trade" and "organic" reflect corporate practices that protect employees and products that safeguard the health of consumers.

- Invest in other women. Microfinance helps women in third-world countries go into business for themselves, ensuring that food appears on their tables for their children.

These and hundreds of other small acts can add up to important changes in our culture. But giving of ourselves economically alone won't cure what ails us. We can't buy our way toward a more just world, and fortunately we don't have to. All we really need to do is be ourselves, our *authentic* selves. Collectively, we women have a God-given inclination to form communities, protect our families, exercise our spirituality, and explore our creativity—pursuits that are, in fact, the perfect antidotes to affluenza.

We have so many opportunities to make a difference right under our own roofs, through our children, in our schools, at the store, and in our backyards. Years ago, before I figured this out, I remember sharing my frustration with a friend. "I just feel helpless in the face of the problems our world faces today," I told her. She said, "You know, Anna, there's only so much you can do." It was a pivotal moment for me, because her statement contained the words I needed to hear. "You are right," I told her, deciding to see the glass as half-full. "There is *so much* I CAN do." Small acts—like growing our own produce; reducing, reusing and recycling; buying local and organic goods; working from home; doing more with less—when added up have the power to transform markets and change lives.

***

Every day we can make a choice to live for a higher purpose. Saint Therese of Lisieux, for example, found that she could express her love for Jesus through small sacrifices on a daily basis. She knew as a Carmelite nun that she would never be able to perform great deeds:

> "Love proves itself by deeds, so how am I to show my love? Great deeds are forbidden me. The only way I can prove my love is by scattering flowers and these flowers are every little sacrifice, every glance and word, and the doing of the least actions for love."[14]

Saint Therese's "Little Way" is the same path we can travel, turning small expressions of generosity toward the earth (turning off the water, turning out the lights) into acts of faith.

Not all that is green is sacrifice and compromise! For me, it's become a fantastic way to save money, get healthy, and protect my family's future. Most of all, it's helped me connect with the inherent

---

14 http://www.catholic.org/saints/saint.php?saint_id=105

beauty of God's natural world, which consistently feeds my creativity and joy. Sustainability is essentially a journey towards simplicity, which has the power to magnify and purify our connection to God while helping us serve his people, too. In fact, it is difficult to build a case against a clear biblical mandate to protect the planet when we read verses like:

> *The land is mine and you are but aliens and my tenants. Throughout the country that you hold as a possession, you must provide for the redemption of the land.* (Leviticus 25:23-24)

or

> *The earth is the Lord's and everything in it.* (Psalms 24:1)

Christian leaders are beginning to open their eyes to the truth and the publishing world is responding. In 2008, HarperOne released the first ever edition of *The Green Bible,* a "green letter" edition of the New Revised Standard Version, containing essays by spiritual leaders such as Jewish ecologist Ellen Bernstein; pastor and activist Brian McLaren; evangelical scientist and ethicist Calvin B. DeWitt; Bishop of Durham for the Church of England N.T. Wright; conservationist, farmer, and poet Wendell Berry; Pope John Paul II; and 13th century Franciscan friar Saint Francis of Assisi. In his essay, James Jones, for example, writes:

> "The only way the earth can be relieved of its curse is through the forgiveness, healing, and restoration of Adam's successors. It is not only Christian, Muslim, and Jewish theologians who would concur with this view. Countless environmentalists, pressure groups, and

lobbyists would testify to the truth that the wholeness of the earth and the future of the planet depend upon the repentance and restoration to wholeness of the human family. You don't have to believe in God to believe the biblical adage, "You reap what you sow." The earth bears the wounds of human sinfulness. "The whole creation has been groaning," says Paul, clinging to the "hope that the creation itself will be set free from its bondage to decay." (Romans 8:21-22)

The Green Bible is a fine example of the kind of interdisciplinary work being developed from all kinds of leaders who are committed to "being the change." In fact, according to Paul Hawken, author of *Blessed Unrest*, organizations focused on restoring the environment and fostering social justice, already constitute the largest movement on earth. A vast number of these organizations have women as their leaders.

Being a "green leader" does not require a public platform so much as personal responsibility from private citizens. Who needs a world stage when a small vegetable patch will do? No act of leadership is too small to make a difference. Revisiting my original question about what "success" means, I'd have to say that these days I think most about a definition attributed to America's legendary naturalist, Ralph Waldo Emerson:

To laugh often and much;
To win the respect of intelligent people and the affection of children;
To earn the appreciation of honest critics and endure the betrayal of false friends;

To appreciate beauty;
To find the best in others;
To leave the world a bit better,
Whether by a healthy child, a garden patch, or a redeemed social condition;
To know even one life has breathed easier because you have lived
This is to have succeeded.

Things may be getting worse, but they are also getting better, and in some ways they are already perfect. Never before have we had so many tools at our disposal to learn, share, influence, and organize to promote fair trade, responsible shopping, toxin-free products, clean energy, and just about anything to protect our environment and each other. Women have an opportunity here. We can use our power, freedom, independence, and affluence as an excuse to fulfill our desires, or we can use our blessings to serve others, our earth, and our God through sacramental acts of simpler living. In my better moments, I choose the latter every chance I get.

Anna Clark is the author of <u>Green, American Style</u>. *She writes on green living, leadership and creation care. She lives with her husband and two children in Dallas, in one of Texas' first residences to earn a platinum-level LEED certification from the U.S. Green Building Council. For more on all things green, visit www.annamclark.com.*

10

Wikiklesia Volume 2 Taking Flight
Opportunities for Seminary-Trained Women: Past, Present, and Future
Vaun Swanson

It has been said that female Christian ministers in the United States today are facing many of the same issues that confronted Viet Nam veterans returning home to the United States in the 1970s. Battle-worn soldiers were met with an ambivalence that has left many of them reeling in confusion and anger even decades later. Similarly, many women graduating from seminaries are finding Christian churches and organizations reluctant to hire them in leadership roles, leaving them angry and confused as well. Now it is not the "war" that is in question. It is the fitness of the "soldier" based on gender alone. Similar to the Viet Nam veterans after the war, however, these women face ambivalence and lack of support from even those closest to them. In fact, the Christian community is deeply divided over whether or not they should even be considered for various service positions in ministry. The respect given to previous generations of Christian ministers and even their male peers is seldom offered to these women.

Why would the Christian community reject or fail to support well-trained female ministers when the apparent need for ministers is so great throughout the world? Why are women entering seminaries when their prospects for vocational ministry are so bleak? This is a multi-faceted issue that requires a close look at the status of seminary-trained women in the U.S., Christian women in American history,

Opportunities for Seminary-Trained Women Vaun Swanson

women in American culture, the religious landscape in America, and the contemporary spirituality of women. We can then look toward the horizon of opportunities for female ministers, examining one example in particular.

The status of seminary-trained women in America

The Barna Research group has investigated gender differences in the American population. Among their findings, women are more likely than men to read the Bible, attend church, pray, be born again, believe the Bible is totally accurate in all of its teachings, and describe themselves as "deeply spiritual."[1] Historically, women have been the backbone of churches.[2] It is only logical that women would desire to attend seminary as a means of better equipping themselves for ministry. Because of the advances women have made in the non-church culture, however, women now expect the same level of respect, compensation, and leadership opportunities afforded men with similar training.

Despite advances women have made in other professions, the Christian culture in America is still struggling to accept women clergy. The *New York Times* reported that women now make up 51 percent of the students in divinity school.[3] Even though women are more prevalent in seminaries, women clergy from every denomination continue to bump up against the "stained-glass ceiling" of longstanding limits, preferences, and prejudices. Finlay's[4] study of seminary students found that female students receive less social support and less material support from family, friends, and churches than male students during seminary.

---

1 "Gender Differences," research archive of The Barna Group, http://www.barna.org (accessed July 28, 2007).
2 Barbara Brown Zikmund, "Women in Ministry Face the '80's," *Christian Century*, February 3-10, 1982, 113.
3 Neela Banerjee, "Clergywomen Find Hard Path to Bigger Pulpit," *The New York Times*, August 26, 2006.
4 Barbara Finlay, *Facing the Stained Glass Ceiling* (Lanham: University Press of America, Inc., 2003), 125.

Women also receive less support than men from congregational members and church officials. In fact, women often experience discrimination, discouragement, and even open hostility from church leaders.

As part of a doctoral thesis project, I surveyed the women who had graduated from Denver Seminary between 1996 and 2006. These were women who had completed M.A. or M.Div. degrees intended to prepare them for ministry in the church or Christian organizations. (I did not include women in the counseling programs, certificate programs, or the D.Min. tracks, nor did I include graduates living outside the United States.) The percentage of female graduates finding appropriate ministry positions was shockingly low. In all, only thirteen percent of the women responding to the survey said that they were working full-time in a ministry position, either within a church or a Christian organization, in which they used their gifts and training and could unqualifiedly sustain themselves financially.

Equally surprising was the fact that nearly half of the women surveyed moved out of their churches or denominations after they enrolled in seminary. It appears that many of the women recognized they would be unable to use their spiritual gifts and training within those churches both during their seminary years and following graduation. Changing churches or denominations during seminary raises new issues, however. The woman is unknown by the congregation and its leaders and is unlikely to have advocates in the new church or denomination. This compounds the difficulty of finding ministry employment as those positions are most often gained through networking and personal relationships. None of the women surveyed found a job through seminary placement services or a job-posting site. The woman is caught in a double-bind: if she stays in her church of origin she is limited by her gender in what she is permitted to do, and if she chooses to leave her home church for a new church she may not be permitted to be fully involved in ministry because she is unknown.[5]

The age at which women were likely to find employment in ministry is another interesting discovery. One might think that age (and the wisdom that presumably comes with age) would be an asset to churches and ministry organizations. The survey results showed just the opposite. None of the women surveyed who were over 49 when they completed seminary was employed in a financially sustainable ministry position. The "Titus Woman" title,[6] often espoused as the duty of older Christian women in evangelical circles, apparently does not translate into formally recognized positions with any economic viability. One has to wonder if older seminary-trained women are viewed as a threat in Christian organizations or if they are merely dismissed as irrelevant.

Overall, the survey findings demonstrated that there is a real problem for women attempting to find suitable ministry positions following graduation from seminary. Lindholm's survey[7] of women who had graduated from Bethel Seminary in San Diego confirmed this phenomenon as well.

Most seminaries accept female students and, in fact, women are heavily recruited by many of them. The placement of women following seminary remains a critical issue, though, as local churches

---

[5] The "brain-drain" from evangelical churches and organizations is great. It seems likely that this will have a negative impact on these institutions in the long run.

[6] Titus 2:3-5: "Likewise, teach the older women to be reverent in the way they live, not to be slanderers or addicted to much wine, but to teach what is good. They can urge the younger women to love their husbands and children, to be self-controlled and pure, to be busy at home, to be kind, and to be subject to their husbands, so that no one will malign the word of God."

[7] Dawn Lindholm, "Report on Ministry Status of Female Graduates of Bethel Seminary/San Diego: 1996-2006" (Doctor of Ministry Project, Gordon-Conwell Theological Seminary, 2007).

generally still prefer male pastors. Lehman[8] studied the placement of both men and women in ministry positions and found that women tended to outperform men grade-wise in seminaries, but men were more successful in finding placement. Male advocacy for women was a key factor for women finding placement. In conservative evangelical seminaries, churches, and denominations it is often difficult for women to find such advocates. Without long-term relationships built with the leaders of their current church it becomes even more unlikely that these women will have clergymen advocates when looking for employment in ministry.[9]

Since some denominations have been ordaining women for full-time clergy roles for decades now, one might think that issues of discrimination would be nonexistent by this time. Carroll, Hargrove, and Lummis[10] discovered otherwise in their study of Mainline protestant denominations. They found that women were more likely than men to be serving in small, rural, and isolated churches or in associate pastor positions throughout their ministry career. While men might start their careers in these positions, they were more likely than women to move on to higher-status and better-paid positions. Similarly, Johnson[11] looked at women clergy in the Evangelical Covenant Church, a denomination that has been open to the ordination of women since 1976. Thirty years later, only nine percent of ordained clergy within the denomination were women, including those that were retired or inactive. Of the 538 clergy members serving as senior or solo pastors, only six percent were women. Johnson concludes that even though the denomination

---

8 Edward C. Lehman, Jr., "Placement of Men and Women in the Ministry," Review of Religious Research 22, no. 1 (September): 18-40.

9 Swanson, 2.

10 Jackson W. Carroll, Barbara Hargrove, and Adair T. Lummis, *Women of the Cloth: A New Opportunity for the Churches* (San Francisco: Harper & Row, 1983).

11 Lenore M. Knight Johnson, "Organic Transformation or Legislated Change? Women's Ordination in the Evangelical Covenant Church" (Master of Arts Thesis, Loyola University, 2005).

approves the ordination of women, parishioners are reluctant to accept women as pastors.

Christian women in American history

A survey of church history leads me to conclude that women were afforded positions of leadership and honor in the early church.[12] Their status in the church and home became more subordinate, however, as the organizational church grew. Hierarchical structures in the church have tended to imitate those in the surrounding culture where men have traditionally assumed positions of power and authority.[13,14]

Throughout most of recorded history women were thought to be inferior to men in every way.[15] In the 1800s, some evangelical women and men openly began to challenge these assumptions, along with assumptions regarding slavery.[16] Women were actively involved as leaders in the abolitionist movement believing that it would grant them freedom as well. Elizabeth Cady Stanton was one of these women.

---

[12] Rodney Stark, *The Rise of Christianity* (U.S.: HarperSanFrancisco, 1997), 107-110.

[13] Ruth A. Tucker and Walter L. Liefeld, *Daughters of the Church: Women and Ministry from New Testament Times to the Present* (Grand Rapids, MI: Zondervan Publishing House, 1987).

[14] E. Margaret Howe, *Women and Church Leadership* (Grand Rapids, MI: Zondervan Publishing House, 1982), 15-27.

[15] John Chrysostom, an early church father (A.D. 347-407), stated that "God maintained the order of each sex by dividing the business of life into two parts, and assigned the more necessary and beneficial aspects to the man and the less important, inferior matters to the woman." *The Kind of Women Who Ought to Be Taken as Wives, IV*, quoted in Elizabeth A. Clark, *Women in the Early Church: Message of the Fathers of the Church*, no. 13 (Wilmington: Glazier, 1983) 37. Francois de Salignac de la Mothe-Fenelon, in *The Education of Females*, published in the late seventeenth century, wrote "A woman's intellect is normally more feeble and her curiosity greater than those of a man ... Women should not govern the state or make war or enter the sacred ministry. Thus they can dispense with some of the more difficult branches of knowledge which deal with politics, the military arts, jurisprudence, philosophy and theology ... Their bodies as well as their minds are less strong and robust than those of men." *Education de Filles* (Paris: E. Flammarion, 1937 reprint), in Osburn, ed., *Essays on Women in Earliest Christianity 2*, 461.

[16] The Seneca Falls, New York convention held in 1848 included evangelical women and men who sought to address the human rights issues of property ownership, child custody, access to education and the right to vote.

Elected as a delegate to the International Anti-slavery Society Convention in London in 1840, she made the lengthy voyage to England. Once there, she was informed that women would not be allowed on the floor of the Convention and was relegated to the balcony, effectively shutting her out of the debate. I can only imagine the anger and disappointment that churned in her soul as she traveled back home. She determined to do everything in her power to call for equal rights for women. She worked with others to plan a gathering to address these issues, resulting in the Seneca Falls Convention in 1848. She also penned the Declaration of Rights and Sentiments, modeled after the Declaration of Independence, changing the opening words ever so slightly to read, "We believe these truths to be self-evident, that all men *and women,* are created equal . . . ."

Over 300 men and women, predominately evangelical Christians, attended the convention and signed the Declaration which affirmed the equality of women and listed the changes that needed to be made in the laws of the country and the practices of the church in order for women to enjoy the freedom and rights afforded men. In reading the Declaration of Rights and Sentiments today one can see that the laws of our country have been changed to give equal rights to women, but the practices of the church remain largely unchanged.

Women in the 1800s began moving outside the church to act on their convictions for social justice. No less than forty-seven independent missions organizations were begun and operated by Christian women in the U.S. Thousands of women were sent out around the world, trained and funded by other women. By the late 1800s, three out of four missionaries on foreign soil were women, often going to the places men refused to go. While the male missionaries were preaching and starting churches, the women were starting schools and hospitals and fighting against unjust practices like foot binding in China and bride burning in India. The male missionaries complained to their denominational mission boards back home that they had no control over what the women missionaries were doing. One by one the women's mission organizations were taken under the umbrellas of denominations and women were once again shut out of leadership by the 1920s.

History really does repeat itself. Women flocked to join the Civil Rights Movement, thinking they could benefit as well. Again, they were shut out of leadership. Angry and determined, a concerted women's movement emerged in the 1960s to challenge inequities, but this time the loudest voices came primarily from secular sources with radical agendas. Conservative church leaders reacted defensively by drawing tighter boundaries around acceptable traditional roles for men and women.[17]

Some evangelical women and men in the 1970s began to question the traditional biblical interpretations used to subordinate women. They were well trained in theology and biblical languages and they saw things in scripture that led them to set forth egalitarian interpretations.[18] In reaction to this, *The Danvers Statement* was drafted in 1987 by The Council on Biblical Manhood and Womanhood, a group of high-profile evangelical leaders led by John Piper and Wayne Grudem.[19]
The *Danvers Statement* was intended to squelch ideas of Christian egalitarianism that were gaining momentum in evangelical circles by stating, among other things, that although men and women are equal before God as persons, they are subject to God-ordained gender roles.

---

17 Tucker and Liefeld, 399.

18 Examples of these writings include Richard Boldrey and Joyce Boldrey, "Women in Paul's Life," *Trinity Studies* 22 (1972) 1-36; Letha Scanzoni and Nancy Hardesty, *All We're Meant to Be* (Waco: Word, 1974); and Patricia Gundry, *Woman Be Free!* (Grand Rapids, MI: Zondervan, 1977).

19 John Piper and Wayne Grudem, ed., *Recovering Biblical Manhood & Womanhood: A Response to Evangelical Feminism* (Wheaton, IL: Crossway Books, 1991), 469-472.

Recovering Biblical Manhood & Womanhood,[20] a sizeable tome on the appropriate roles for men and women, followed shortly thereafter.

The lines were now drawn and denominations and seminaries were pressured to take a stand. Several denominations effectively closed their doors to women in leadership positions.[21] A few made controversial decisions to open their doors to women pastors and leaders.[22] Many seminaries, needing the tuition payments of the growing ranks of female students, typically refused to come down on one side or the other.

Pierce and Groothuis published *Discovering Biblical Equality: Complementarity without Hierarchy* in 2004[23] and this book challenged, chapter-by-chapter, the Piper and Grudem book mentioned above. Many books, both popular and scholarly, have been written from both sides of the complementarian/egalitarian[24] issue, fueling the debate.

---

20 Ibid.

21 The Southern Baptist Convention, the largest protestant denomination in the U.S., has historically been largely opposed to the ordination of women but would allow individual Southern Baptist churches to ordain women. The first ordination of an SBC woman took place in 1964. In June of 1984 the SBC voted to deny women ordination in order "to preserve a submission God requires because man was first in creation and woman was first in the Edenic fall." In C. Robert Wetzel, ed., *Essays on New Testament Christianity* (Cincinnati: Standard, 1978). The "Baptist Faith and Message" statement arising out of the 2000 Baptist General Conference includes a statement that pastors are to be men. Because those teaching theology in SBC schools are considered to be pastors, women are no longer permitted to teach theology in these schools. Other denominations that have closed their doors to the ordination of women in the past 35 years include the Evangelical Free Church of America, The Christian and Missionary Alliance, and the Missouri Synod Lutheran.

22 The American Lutheran Church, the Lutheran Church in America, the Christian Reformed Church, and the Evangelical Covenant Church are all examples of denominations that have opened their doors to women clergy since the 1970s.

23 Ronald W. Pierce and Rebecca Merrill Groothuis, eds., Gordon D. Fee, contributing ed., *Discovering Biblical Equality: Complementarity Without Hierarchy* (Downers Grove, IL: IVP, 2004).

24 "Complementarian" is the preferred title of those who adhere to the belief that God has ordained distinct roles for men and women that are complementary but also obligate women to be in submission to men. Other titles used for adherents to this belief are "traditionalist" and "hierarchicalist." Egalitarians believe that men and women complement each other but are functionally and ontologically equal.

In May of 2007 the Gospel Coalition was organized, spearheaded by forty theologians and pastors (including outspoken complementarians D. A. Carson, Tim Keller, John Piper and Mark Driscoll). Their goal is a renewed evangelical commitment to core confessional beliefs, including a belief that men are to lead churches and homes.[25] Trinity Evangelical Divinity School, which continues to recruit and educate women for ministry, provided the initial funding for the Gospel Coalition. For female seminarians, the ambiguity continues.

Women in American culture

American culture is telling women that they can do anything they choose. Women made up the majority of medical school applicants for the first time in 2003,[26] and forty-seven percent of law school students are women.[27] The earning power of women in their twenties is now 117 percent of men's wages in major cities around the country.[28] Women today have far more opportunities open to them than even a generation ago, and they are stepping into them in force.

In many ways the American culture and the Christian culture are moving further apart. While the conservative Christian culture is still championing men as the spiritual heads of the home and the primary wage-earners, the number of stay-at-home fathers in the U.S. has tripled in the past ten years. When ranking marriage, parenthood, and job in terms of priority, Generation X men put their job dead last. What has

---

25 Collin Hansen, "Tethered to the Center: The Gospel Coalition is committed to core evangelical beliefs and wide-ranging cultural engagement," *Christianity Today*, October 2007, 70-71.

26 "Applicants to U.S. Medical Schools Increase: Women the Majority for the First Time," Association of American Medical Colleges press release, Washington, D.C., November 4, 2003, http://www.aamc.org//newsroom/pressrel/2003/031104.htm (accessed May 7, 2008).

27 Leigh Jones, "Fewer Women are Seeking Law Degrees," *The National Law Journal*, October 2, 2007.

28 Jen Chung, "Young Women in Cities: You're Gonna Make it After All," *Gothamist*, August 3, 2007, http://gothamist.com/2007/0803/girl_youre_gonn.php (accessed May 7, 2008).

been the most masculine of roles—going out into the world to work—is receding in importance for younger men.[29]

Paradoxically, there has been an increasing amount of emphasis placed on a woman's body. Just look at the recent media attention given to Sarah Palin and Michelle Obama. For women, clothing and hairstyles, weight gain or loss, and make-up are all subject to commentary by almost everyone, adding to the difficulties women still face.

"Everyone I knew in High School threw up after lunch," a young woman told me recently. In the United States, eating disorders (anorexia, bulimia, binge eating) are more common than Alzheimer's disease (5-10 million people have eating disorders compared to 4 million with Alzheimer's disease).[30] In a study of Division 1 NCAA athletes, over one-third of female athletes reported attitudes and symptoms placing them at risk for anorexia nervosa. On the flip side, on average, American women consume 344 more calories per day than they did in 1974. Sixty-one percent of women today are overweight, compared with 41% in the 1970s.[31]

Though girls begin their lives feeling happier and more fulfilled than boys, as they age, their happiness decreases, while men get happier as they get older. The trajectory for women is consistent, and consistently downhill. By almost all measures, life is getting better for women, yet the World Health Organization reports that depression has become the second most debilitating disease for women (heart disease is first). There is no doubt that American women are feeling stressed.

---

29 Lisa Takeuchi Cullen and Lev Grossman, "Fatherhood 2.0," *Life*, October 15, 2007, 63-66.

30 NationalEatingDisorders.org.

31 *Time*, Special Report on Women, 2009.

Psychologist Ani Ligget describes midlife women in her practice as exhibiting the classic symptoms of Failure to Thrive Syndrome. She interviewed 20 of these women for her book and they all said something like "I felt like I was dying." It was at this point that these women began to look for more authenticity in their lives, including a re-examination of their spirituality.[32] Before looking more closely at the spirituality of women, let's sidestep for a moment to look at religion in America.

The religious landscape in America

The overall religious landscape in America is changing rapidly. Pew Forum studies show that younger Americans tend to be considerably less Protestant and less religiously affiliated than older Americans. In fact, one quarter of all adults under age thirty are not affiliated with any particular religion. Twenty percent of adults who were reared as Protestants have forsaken Protestantism.[33] Barna predicts that the percentage of people who rely on the local church as their primary means of spiritual experience and expression will drop from 70 percent in 2000 to 30-35 percent in 2025.[34]

Non-denominational evangelical churches are the largest growth subset of Protestant churches in America having gained the most new members from other denominations. Overall, nearly one in ten Protestants was reared in the Catholic Church, a large number of these people presumably migrating to non-denominational churches. The non-denominational charismatic, evangelical, and fundamentalist church members also have the highest number of children in their homes, making the overall demographics of these churches much

---

32 Ann Liggett, *Endings, Beginnings....When Midlife Women Leave Home In Search of Authenticity* (Lafayette, CO: BeMe Press, 2009).

33 The Pew Forum on Religion & Public Life/U.S. Religious Landscape Survey, http://pewforum.org (accessed October 22, 2008).

34 George Barna, *Revolution* (U.S.: Tyndale House Publishers, 2005), 49.

younger than traditional denominational churches. These non-denominational churches will likely lead the way for Protestants in the coming years, yet these are the very churches that are often closed to the full expression of the spiritual gifts and leadership of women. Currently, the largest denominations in the U.S. are the Roman Catholic Church and the Southern Baptist Convention, both of which place limitations on women.

The spirituality of women

Something else is going on in American spirituality in the twenty-first century: nineteen million American women are entering menopause. Many of these women have been active in the feminist movement and they are now casting off patriarchal religions and redefining themselves spiritually. Popular author, Sue Monk Kidd, describes her personal journey in this direction in *The Dance of the Dissident Daughter*[35] and her more recent publication, *Traveling With Pomegranates,*[36] co-authored with her daughter, Ann Kidd Taylor. Social researcher Paul Ray has identified a subculture of forty-four million people, or 24 percent of the American adult population, whose values center on spirituality, self-actualization, self-expression, ecology, and elevation of the feminine to a new place in recent human history. Twice as many women as men are involved in this subculture. "It is deeply concerned with reintegration of what has been fragmented by modernism: self, authenticity, connection with community and nature, and tolerance for diverse views and traditions. According to Ray's research, this subculture is not a fringe phenomenon, but is very much a part of mainstream American life."[37] American women are increasingly attracted to the Goddess because she

---

35 Sue Monk Kidd, *The Dance of the Dissident Daughter*

36 Sue Monk Kidd and Ann Kidd Taylor, *Traveling With Pomegranates: A Mother-Daughter Story* (U.S.A.: Viking Penguin, 2009).

37 Liggett, 170.

provides a model of feminine strength, beauty, and freedom they are not finding in Christianity.

A sampling of the ancient and contemporary expressions of women's spirituality which are blossoming today include Ecopsychology, Voluntary Simplicity, Ecofeminism, Paganism, Wicca, and Native American Spirituality. The Virgin Mary and Mary Magdalene are also re-emerging as personifications of the Divine Feminine. The Black Madonnas of Europe have become popular travel and worship destinations for American women. The Life-Coaching and Motivational Speaking professions are steeped in Western Buddhism where women are now playing predominant teaching roles. The Conscious Aging Movement affirms the importance of the elder years for women and includes gatherings such as the annual Crones Counsel and Sage-ing Centers.

One thing seems clear: if Christ-followers want to relate to these women they are going to need to develop a new language and new means of expression. Patriarchal and hierarchical language and religious institutions will no longer be tolerated.

On the horizon

All signs point to a dramatic reshaping of the business, religious, and social institutions of western culture in years to come. Much of that reshaping will come about through the efforts of those currently on the fringes of existing institutions. The people on the margins are waiting for the opportunity to play a meaningful role in communities that they can help to shape and improve. It is time for women to rise up and join together in creating and funding these new organizations.

In order to connect with women in American culture, Christ-following communities will need to embrace the positive values of the emerging American culture-at-large, which include equality; social justice; collaboration rather than hierarchy; artistic expression; authentic living that integrates the body, mind, and soul; simple living; creation care; the honoring of diversity; open conversation; and community. All of these values are consistent with the teachings of Jesus.

If ever there was a need for well-trained female ministers it is now. We need to stop behaving like victims, though, and take responsibility for finding new ways to use our influence in the world and minister to people while sustaining ourselves financially. Women are the future of the church in America. A few women are already bravely stepping outside the traditional church and Christian ministry paradigms to begin this work, but many more are needed. It is likely that these women will continue to face ambivalence and lack of support from traditional Christians. But just as our foremothers, we must band together and move forward in bringing the tangible love and justice of Christ to our world.

Pomegranate Place

Pomegranate Place is one example of an alternative setting for Christian women to freely use their gifts, skills, and training in the community. It is like a watering hole for a diverse group of women to gather, exchange ideas, and collaborate. Housed in an historic mansion in Denver, Colorado, Pomegranate Place has the heart of a sanctuary and the warmth of a spa, providing a safe place for women to grow and thrive. Skilled and trained women from a variety of professions (including seminary trained ministers) facilitate workshops, retreats, and classes. We also offer informal gathering space, a coffee bar, book studies, life coaching, mentoring, spiritual direction, art classes, writing workshops, and reflection gardens.[38]

Women are constantly bombarded with balancing home life and career, while, at the same time, longing for a sense of belonging and purpose. Our mission is to provide opportunities for women to discover and live out the purposes for which they were created. In doing this, we are watching women come alive to possibilities in their lives and finding avenues to use their gifts in service to others. We are also creating a web of women who are historically among the most well-educated, wealthy, powerful women who have ever walked the face of this earth. We anticipate that as we heal and grow individually, we will collaborate and encourage one another to face the challenges of our world head-on.

Enlisting the help of non-Christ-following women in the formative stages of Pomegranate Place has been extremely valuable. After spending a lifetime in the Christian community I find myself needing to learn to speak a new language. I am being challenged and stretched in new ways and constantly feeling the need to recalibrate my direction. I am daily reminded of the prayer of Thomas Merton: "My Lord God I have no idea where I am going. I do not see the road ahead of me . . . But I believe that my desire to please you does in fact please you."

Conclusion

It is clear that American culture and the American church are following divergent paths regarding women. American culture is liberating women at the same time the church is systematically holding them back. Power struggles over what women can and cannot do are playing out in churches and denominations that are becoming more

---
38 Visit www.pomegranateplace.org for more information.

irrelevant to the culture-at-large every day. Seminary-trained women are caught in a vicious crossfire that very few anticipated when they responded to God's call to become better equipped for ministry in the Kingdom of God. Far too many good women are not finding ministry positions that will both utilize their training and abilities and support them financially. Rather than continuing to bang on the doors of these old religious structures, women need to work together to discover viable alternative ministry paths in which they will thrive in the use of their gifts and training. Trained female ministers are needed to address the serious spiritual, emotional, and physical issues women in America are facing. Women need to pull their financial support from patriarchal and hierarchical Christian churches and organizations and invest it in those that affirm their equality. With God's help, and the leadership of gifted and skilled women ministers who have been set free, we can change our world for the better.

Vaun Swanson, D.Min., has served in helping professions for the past 30 years as a social worker, church-planter, pastor, short-term missionary and mentor for seminary students and ministry professionals. She now offers opportunities for women to connect and grow at Pomegranate Place, a community center she recently founded for women in Denver, Colorado. Vaun has been married to Barry since 1977 and they have three grown sons. Visit www.pomegranateplace.org

Innovation often originates outside existing organizations, in part because successful organizations acqure a commitment to the status quo and a resistance to ideas that might change it.
--- Nathan Rosenberg

Wikiklesia Volume 2 Taking Flight
The Sophia Network: Activists for Change
Jenny Baker

The privilege of privilege is that the terms of privilege are rendered invisible. It is a luxury not to have to think about race, or class, or gender. Only those marginalized by some category understand how powerful that category is when deployed against them.[1]

I grew up in the Brethren Church in the UK, where the roles of men and women were neatly divided—men made the decisions and women made the tea. A formative memory from my teenage years was of a woman who stood up in the Sunday morning service and started reading the story of Rahab. About ten people got up and walked out because they were so offended. When she reached the end of the Bible passage, one of the elders ended her bid for equality with a weary, "I think that's enough Audrey, dear," so she sat down and shut up.

As I got older I oscillated between thinking, "If that's what God wants for men and women then I shall put up with it because I want to follow God," and "If that's what God wants, then I want nothing to do with God." Shortly before I got married, I joined a study group in a different church that was taking a fresh look at passages about gender

---

[1] Michael S. Kimmel, "Why men should support gender equity", Women's Studies Review, Fall 2005

in the Bible. Some months of wrestling with theology ensued but I came to a very different understanding of what the Bible said about men and women and our place in salvation history.

I became a youth worker just over 20 years ago, working for Youth for Christ in Bath. Shortly afterwards, I was appointed Director of the centre there, and then when we had children my husband and I job-shared and shared the hands-on parenting of our two sons—an incredibly rewarding time. I was aware that I was a bit of an anomaly as a woman in youth ministry, and even more so as one in leadership—there weren't many of us around. Fast forward 20 years and conversations with friends and colleagues made me realize that I was taking for granted the supportive environment of my church and work context and that I should look with fresh eyes at the youth ministry scene in the UK. There are lots more women in youth ministry, and there's a pretty even gender-split among students in Christian youth work courses, but there are still very few women in positions of leadership and responsibility in youth organizations, very few involved in strategic direction and shaping the future. It felt in many ways like little had changed from my Brethren days, and so a few of us set up the Sophia Network for women in youth work and ministry to try and address the imbalance.

Our conviction is that God created men and women to work together in partnership. The first thing in all creation that was not good was that the man was alone, and so God created woman. Together they were given the cultural mandate to fill all the earth and subdue the land, the task of unlocking the potential of creation and bringing new things to birth. Where women are missing or their voices are silenced, or where men are absent or excluded, then the body of Christ is impoverished, the image of God in humanity is diminished, and we can end up misrepresenting the gospel, particularly to young people outside of the church who grow up with equality as a given. We need to actively work at breaking down barriers, challenging unhelpful stereotypes and enabling both men and women to reach their full potential. Our ultimate aim is to encourage women and men to work together more closely in a way that reflects the heart of God, but we recognize that sometimes issues need to be addressed before women can contribute on a level playing field.

The Sophia Network for women in youth work and ministry was set up in the UK in November 2007, beginning with an online presence. It takes time to change the culture of the church and organizations and to get individuals to rethink their views, but these are some of the ways we are trying to make a difference.

Providing a sense of solidarity for women in youth ministry

Shortly after we launched, we did a survey of youth workers asking what were the key issues facing women in youth work. One of the most striking themes that emerged was women looking for permission to work and minister. The overarching question that they seemed to be asking was, 'Am I allowed to do this, and am I allowed to do it well?'

A friend of mine is a female Church of England vicar in a town just north of London. New to the area, she asked to meet with a local Baptist minister to find out what his church did and to explore whether there were any ways in which they could work together. He would only meet her if his wife was present as well, and he then proceeded to tell her that he couldn't work with her because she was 'in sin' as a woman in leadership. My friend first felt a call to ministry many years ago and has had the call recognized by her local church and by the national church who accepted her for ordination. She spent three years studying and three years as a curate, with her vocation affirmed along the way, and yet this conversation with this man shook her to the core and made her question whether she was doing the right thing. I don't think she's alone in that.

Studies have documented the effect that stereotypes have on performance. Psychologist Sian Beilock recruited some female university students and asked them to take a math test.[2] One group of students was told that the purpose of the research was to understand why men in general do better than women at math; the others were just asked to do the test. The women in the first group who were reminded of the stereotype that women are worse at math did worse in the test, getting 10-15% fewer marks. Beilock argued that they were responding to "stereotype threat," allowing anxiety to stop them from succeeding because they know that they're expected to fail. The same result was gained with elderly people who were asked to do a memory test. Those who were reminded that memory declines with age proved more forgetful.

The knowledge that some people within the church think that women are inferior and their contribution should be restricted can be surprisingly undermining for even the most confident women, but even more so for women starting out in ministry. When my friend's vocation was dismissed by that man, when women are told that they can't lead or teach, the sisterhood takes a hit. One of the key roles that I think the Sophia Network can play is to say, "We believe in you. You are allowed to do this and you're allowed to do it well. Here is a like-minded community of women in leadership and ministry who are doing similar things; if you need permission, then here, have it."

---

2 http://www.guardian.co.uk/lifeandstyle/2008/apr/26/healthandwellbeing.oliverburkeman - Accessed 4 August 2009

Increasing the visibility of women

Since the launch of the network, we have challenged event organizers, editors, and resource producers where they have included few or no women. Invariably the response is, "We'd like to include more women, but we don't know any!" Many women are caught in the vicious circle of not being invited to contribute—if you don't have experience then you're not trusted to speak; if you're not invited to speak then you never gain experience.

In 2008, it became a legal requirement in Norway that women should comprise 40% of non-executive directors on the boards of companies over a certain size. The quota was introduced as a voluntary measure first, but when it didn't produce change quickly enough it was made compulsory. Of course it was incredibly controversial with claims that competent men would have to be replaced by inadequate women, and lots of companies saying that they just couldn't find women with experience to fill the places on their boards. One recruitment consultant held a press conference where she said nothing, just showed the CVs of 100 proficient women who could fill any number of the vacancies.[3] The problem was not that the women existed; it was that the men didn't know them. She went on to talk about what is known as the "grey men's club" in Norway, the all-male networks that perpetuate the mostly-male business world, and how the quotas forced men to look beyond their magic inner-circle. I suspect that the same is true of the church that prides itself on its relationality but doesn't quite know how to cope with working relationships between men and women. We want to encourage gatekeepers who can provide opportunities for women to speak, write, and lead to take some risks and not just go for the safe pair of hands.

---

[3] http://www.guardian.co.uk/lifeandstyle/2008/mar/06/women.discriminationatwork – Accessed 4 August 2009

The Sophia Network: Activists for Change   Jenny Baker

So, we include interviews with women in youth work and ministry on our website and have the beginnings of a speakers list that we can send out to people who don't know any women to invite—and we want to develop that more. We have recommended female youth workers for ministry teams at events and for local preaching opportunities. We've organized gatherings at festivals and conferences, we have a members' directory on the website and some regional meetings are getting off the ground, all providing the essential networking that will increase the knowledge of the fantastic, gifted, prophetic women who are currently missing from the table.

Encouraging a healthy understanding of gender and how it affects our lives

Humanity isn't divided into two neat, distinct, homogeneous groups—one male and one female. All kinds of factors affect the kind of people we become, not just our sex. There can be as much difference between two girls as there can be between a boy and a girl because of their upbringing, relationships with parents, class, ethnicity, education, and so on. That's why it's more accurate to talk about "masculinities" and "femininities," rather than using the terms in the singular. Within any culture, there are lots of different ways of being masculine, for example, some of which have more status and power than others.

If you read some of the material written about gender by Christians, though, you'll get a very different picture of God creating us in particular moulds with all men having some characteristics and all women having others, and woe unto anyone who doesn't fit! The reality is that gender is far more complex than that, and if we're enthralled with gender stereotypes we can end up justifying immaturity and perpetuating damaging behavior. Recent research in the UK, for example, has shown that men are significantly more likely to both get cancer and to die from it.[4] There's no biological reason why that should be so; men's bodies are not more susceptible to cancer than women's. It's thought to be linked to stereotypical behavior such as men not being as health conscious as women and so more prone to risks that lead to cancer, or men down-playing early symptoms and being reluctant to visit doctors and ask for advice. Rather than upholding stereotypes, perhaps we need to critique and subvert them, especially if people's lives are at risk.

The blog on our website highlights gender issues that are in the news and points people toward recent research. We try to help people navigate the complexity of the issues and the ways in which both women and men can suffer from inequality and discrimination. And we aim to point out where other factors such as class, ethnicity, and disability can combine with gender to increase disadvantage or accelerate potential, depending on who you are.

Increasing the skills and confidence of women in ministry

It's not only the church that suffers from a gender imbalance in leadership. In the UK, the arts are also missing women in positions of responsibility and vision. A national newspaper list of the 100 most influential people in culture in 2008 included just 18 women with only three in the top 20.[5] One of the contributing factors to the lack of women in influential positions is thought to be their self-doubt. A consultant who regularly sits on arts appointment panels says that all candidates are psychometrically tested, and "you can always guess whether a candidate is male or female. The characteristics that are flagged up again and again for the women are: self-doubt, questioning their ability to lead, and reluctance to step forward for promotion. It all adds up to

---

[4] http://www.menshealthforum.org.uk/userpage1.cfm?item_id=2817 – Accessed 4 August 2009

[5] http://www.telegraph.co.uk/culture/3672604/The-100-most-powerful-people-in-British-culture-1-20.html – Accessed 4 August 2009

a weaker sense of female entitlement for those very senior jobs."[6] Of course there's a huge diversity of women within the church but I think that same doubt can affect some Christian women too, and it's something I'm keen for us to address through training and creating opportunities for women to flourish.

The other major finding from the survey we did after our launch was that many women were looking for mentors, people further ahead of them in life who could provide advice, skills, opportunities, and support. Many of them were also looking for guidance on how to mentor others, particularly the younger women that they worked with. There was a sense that people wanted to make things easier for those who came behind them, to provide the role models and support that they had missed early on in their ministry. We've developed mentoring training and raised money to put it on around the country. Next year, we're partnering with a youth organization that will enable us to serve far more venues and reach more people. Our emphasis is on women being proactive about getting the support that they need, not just sitting and hoping that things will change. We've put on communication skills training, high-quality events with an experienced actress and voice coach who can guide us in effective communication and to help us avoid being taken in by the blokey, shouty style of preaching that we so often equate with anointing.

We've also encouraged Tearfund, a Christian relief and development agency, to provide immersion trips for women leaders to see what life is like for women in a developing country, and to have an adventure while they're doing it. In January 2009, three Sophia members joined six other women on an unforgettable trip to Cambodia where we visited projects working in villages and in the church. A Cambodian

---

6 http://www.guardian.co.uk/artanddesign/2008/jun/09/art.women – Accessed 4 August 2009

saying is that men are like gold and women are like flowers. We saw how cultural values like this affect the lives of women, for instance it's considered rude for a woman to turn her back on her husband in bed. Sadly, these values also play out within the church. But we also spent a night in a village with a woman who was HIV positive, and experiencing her day-to-day life was such a privilege. We went way outside our comfort zones and had many conversations about what we had to offer the kingdom of God as individuals and together. Those of us who suffer from self-doubt came back determined to conquer it and to just get on with what God is calling us to. In 2010, Tearfund is doing a similar trip to Malawi and we'll be urging Sophia members to go.

Keeping up the conversation

In summer 2009, we held a consultation on how churches and organizations can be places where both women and men thrive in ministry. At lunch a church leader approached me and asked, "If I believe in male eldership in the church and male headship in the home, am I a block to equality?" I swallowed my initial response to that question, and instead we talked about the different views of equality we held and the importance of listening to and including women, whatever one's theological perspective. His parting words to me were that he felt all churches needed to consider issues of equality and gender, and that the Sophia Network needed to keep the conversation open and not alienate people by identifying too closely with one "camp."

I'm still thinking about his words, but we have deliberately chosen from the start not to have a "statement of faith" or a theological "position" so that we don't alienate those who might hold different views. It's clear from our website that we support and encourage women in leadership through the articles we publish and the events we put on, and the people on our steering group all hold a broadly egalitarian theology, but I hope we can provide space for everyone to consider the issues and listen to each other.

A female priest who also attended the consultation, wrote to me afterwards about how she had come to the conclusion that the efforts of the Church of England to keep on board the opponents of the ordination of women, as painful and unfair as they have felt at times, have been a better option than allowing it to cause a complete split. She said, "Having a space which is trying to allow for all shades of opinion about a woman's place in the church while promoting our equality as people in God's sight has got to be better than saying 'unless you see it like I do, you aren't worth talking to.' I think eventually people start to build relationship and listen to each other if the lines of communication are open."

And what we need to do better

The Sophia Network is still very young and we have been amazed at the response we have had—people are resonating with what we are doing. Something is stirring in the body of Christ and more and more of us are not satisfied with the status quo. There's a hunger for justice and liberation, and an end to the competition that so often characterizes relationships between men and women. We have already stretched beyond our original target audience of female youth workers and have church leaders, children's workers, worship leaders, and others in ministry among our members. We need to think about how we cater to the different needs represented within each arena of work. But there's a lot more that we could do, and I think this is the most pressing issue:

To find men who will speak up for the equality of men and women

Historically it has always been women who have agitated for change and equality. None of the key freedoms and opportunities that are now available to women through science and technology, economic transformation, educational opportunity, or the political process have been the result of men initiating change or, some would argue, men changing themselves.[7] But we will never get far enough without men also on this journey. Part of that is pragmatic; some men will never listen to a woman talking about the need for a change in theological thinking precisely because of their theology. We need men who can speak into those arenas where women will never be heard. But it's also ideological. We believe that God created men and women to work in partnership, so it makes no sense for women to go it alone. We need to model what we value.

However, membership of the Sophia Network is only open to women for a number of reasons—partly so that we can take positive action as women on the issues that we face rather than expecting or hoping someone else will sort it out; partly so that the members' area can be a safe place where women can discuss the issues that concern them; partly to raise awareness and to be a catalyst for people to think through the issues. Men who support our aims can become Friends of Sophia and get all the same benefits, apart from access to the members' area. Is that enough? Does that create a two-tier system that implies that men are somehow secondary in this work towards equality, or worse that they are all part of the problem just because they are men? We need to keep talking that through and to seek the wisdom of God for the way ahead.

---

7 Whitehead, S and Barrett, F, 2001. *The Masculinities Reader*. Cambridge: Polity, p5

The Sophia Network: Activists for Change Jenny Baker

Thoughts for the future

Recently I was asked to contribute to a special edition of Youthwork magazine in the UK, which asked activists and leaders within youth work and ministry to envision what they want to see happen within the next ten years in their area of focus. This is how I ended my piece:

> "In ten years time, I want to see a woman as CEO of a major Christian youth organization, because she's a woman of integrity, vision, and experience and was the best person for the job.
>
> I want it to be unacceptable and inconceivable for Christian conferences, churches, and university CUs to not make room for women's voices on an equal basis to men's as speakers and leaders, for there to be a vast and visible pool of talented, competent women to choose from, and for audiences to have been educated beyond the narrow and very male style of speaking that we so often equate with "hearing from God."
>
> I want young people to have strong role models of their own sex that show them what it is to be men and women of God, and how to have healthy, respectful, empowering relationships with the opposite sex. I want youth work to meet the gender-specific needs of young people in a way that enables them to reach their full potential instead of boxing them into stereotypical roles that constrain and deaden them.

And I hope that the Sophia Network doesn't exist in ten years' time, that there's no longer any need to speak up for women in ministry because we'll all be free to use our gifts and follow our callings in the work of the kingdom.

Jenny Baker is a writer and a co-founder of the Sophia Network for women in youth work and ministry. She is a triathlete and a trustee of the Greenbelt Festival, and is currently studying for a Masters in Gender, Sexuality and Society. She lives in London, England with her husband and two sons where she is a member of Grace, an alternative worship community at St Mary's Ealing. Visit www.sophianetwork.org.uk

Far away there in the sunshine are my highest aspirations.
I may not reach them, but I can look up and see their beauty,
believe in them, and try to follow where they lead.
--- Louisa May Alcott

Wikiklesia Volume 2 Taking Flight

Shoulders to Stand On: Men's Role in Restoring the Woman's Voice

Jeff McQuilkin

There's a well-respected pastor in our town with whom I've shared lunch numerous times—an elderly man with many "war stories." He shared with me once about how he had been part of the historic civil rights march in Alabama from Selma to Montgomery in 1965. His passion was apparent in telling the story of his participation. What struck me most about his story was that he is a white man.

When we remember those turbulent times, we typically recall the pictures of the oppressed African-Americans standing up bravely for their right to be treated as equals. What we don't often hear about are the numerous white people who came alongside the African-Americans, marched with them, and stood in solidarity with them, often at great personal risk. Yet their presence went a long way toward weakening the strangleholds of racism in this nation. There is something very powerful and spiritual that happens when members of an oppressing group cross the boundary and begin lifting up the oppressed.

As we know, however, racial issues are not the only inequity found in our culture. Gender equality has been a long-standing issue as well. The struggle for "women's rights" in our culture is now well over a century old, and while there has admittedly been much progress during that time, it still appears that the change of heart required to utterly defeat sexism has been slower in coming. On one hand, women have won the right to vote and hold office, to be doctors and lawyers and professional athletes and soldiers—all of which were at one time considered "man's territory." On the other hand, women are still frequently subjected to demeaning remarks in the workplace, still overlooked for promotions, still paid less than their male counterparts in many cases, and still unfairly disqualified from certain roles by subtle politics. And in many church settings, the "overlooking" is backed up by (mis)using the authority of Scripture. It all still happens, primarily because while times have changed, many people have not. There are still many men, both in the church and out, who claim to have "no problem" with women, but who still carry a subtle (or not-so-subtle) belief in male superiority.

So why, after all this time and all the contending women have done over the years, why is it still such an uphill climb for them? And even more importantly—what is to be done about it?

As a Christ-follower, I believe *restoration* is a huge part of what Jesus came to do—to restore the broken relationship between God and humans, and to restore the elements of our lives that had been broken by the fall of man. I believe that restoration includes restoring the female half of God's image to what God intended her to be—and this includes freeing her from shackles of suppression and silence, restoring her status, and her voice. Thus, despite the long-standing misinterpretations of Scripture to keep women in an inferior position, and despite the accusations of traditionalists that Christians who favor the equality of women are bowing to the demands of modern-day feminism and popular culture—if we are to be true to the heart of restoration in the ministry of Christ, then the church should actually lead the way in restoring women to their God-given status. When we do so, we aren't compromising Scripture to be popular with the world—we are participating in the mission of Christ.

Even so, it's apparent from the continued resistance women face that they are not going to make this restoration happen by themselves. There must be something more. If the example of Christ is any indication, it's going to take godly men coming alongside their sisters and taking an active role in their restoration. I'd like to share some thoughts on how we can effectively do this. And because I believe the church should be at the forefront of restoration, most of my remarks going forward will be directed toward Christ-followers and gender relationships in the church.

Ways men add to the problem

Speaking as a man, before we can become part of the solution here, we first need to understand the ways in which we are still part of the problem. This isn't always as obvious to us men as it might appear, because the signs of sexism are often more subtle in our culture than they used to be. So here are a couple of ways we often make things worse, perhaps without realizing it:

1. Passivity and passive resistance. While most men nowadays probably don't *purposefully* oppose women in places formerly reserved for men, neither do they do anything to enable or support them. In the church it is no different. Men won't necessarily leave the room anymore, or turn their backs when a woman speaks publicly in church, but when it comes to the resistance women still face in a male-dominated society, those women are still pretty much left on their own. Men will often "be okay" with women having positions of leadership, for example, but will do nothing to include them. Excuses are made when women continue to be overlooked: "There weren't any women qualified to do this;" "No women applied for the position;" "It just happened this way, no one intentionally excluded women." These excuses usually are spoken with a *what's-the-big-deal* tone in our voice, which basically means we're more concerned with *appearing* to be open-minded than we are in truly understanding the problem. This passive approach is a subtle form of sexism, simply because the resistance against women is a default of our culture, and if we don't purposefully lean against it, we find ourselves in a place of passive resistance. Our sisters need more from us than this.

2. Expecting women to function as men. Let's go ahead and state the obvious: men and women are different. When we say they are *equal,* we are not saying they are *identical.* God makes us with different sets of strengths: men tend to be physically stronger than women, while women tend to be more intuitive and detail-oriented. (This is a generalization, of course, with exceptions on both sides. There are numerous women out there who could beat the snot out of me—and some who might want to!—and there are also many men who are highly intuitive.)

The problem is that for so long, both in and out of the church, this has been a "man's world" and consequently we often define a role or vocation by male strengths. So when a woman enters the workforce, it is often demanded that she "keep up" with the men—meaning she is expected to function the same way a man would in that role, rather than as a woman, at the risk of being considered inadequate to the job description.

But if women truly have the same right to function in a public capacity, then it follows that *women should not have to become men* in order to be qualified. Rather, they should be allowed to handle their tasks according to their own strengths and abilities. In other words, the role should be ultimately defined by the person, not by the gender.

By extension, in the church, leadership is not a "man's job," it is simply a function. A woman who fulfills that function in the church is not trying to fill a man's shoes, and should not be expected to. She fills her own shoes, bringing her own set of gifts to that role, and that should be respected. When we men think otherwise—when we treat a woman in leadership like she is filling in for a man, or expect her to "harden up" like a man before we respect her—we are adding to the soul-numbing resistance she experiences. And make no mistake, this happens all the time.

Why men must become part of the solution

Once we learn to stop being part of the problem, the next step of restoration is for men to come alongside the women and actively support and defend them. I think this is important for several reasons.

First—men must be part of the healing process, because men are the ones who have done the damage. It is a principle found in Scripture, and in fact part of God's justice, that those who have done harm must make restitution. The alienation so many women feel because of men in general is greater than we care to admit; and that will not go away simply because men decide to stop being sexist, nor will it go away by women preferring one another. Men have done the wounding, so only men can do the healing. That healing comes, not just by ceasing to do wrong to our sisters, but by purposefully finding ways to show them honor and preference.

As an illustration, if gender relations were placed on a number line with zero at the center, the long-standing suppression of women and their gifts has placed us well into negative territory. Simple logic says we cannot go into positive territory simply by ceasing to go the wrong direction. It is going to take some traveling back across the negative territory to get back into the positive area. That will take time, patience, and a consistent pattern of different behavior and attitudes. Thus, it requires men who are willing to *un*do the damage that men have done. Even if as a man you have never been part of inflicting the wound (a highly unlikely prospect), as a man you have the ability to bring healing. We need to do it, because we can.

Second—in a man's world, a man's voice is still considered the voice of authority. It isn't right, but it is reality. Put bluntly, the men who are still carrying sexist attitudes are not going to listen to the women advocating for themselves. If they are going to listen to anyone, it is going to be other men. This is where men must be advocates, those who will stand up for the plight of another—in this case, our sisters.

Going back to the story I shared at the beginning of this chapter—my white pastor friend participated in the Selma march because he wanted to be part of the solution for the oppressed black population and he knew that the voice of the white man would carry more weight among those doing the oppressing. By the same token, in a male-dominated world where a woman's voice is still barely heard, the voice that *will* be listened to is still a man's. And it's no different in a male-dominated *church*. Where the woman's voice has been silenced, godly men need to speak for their sisters.

Ways we can be part of the solution

I'm a thinker and a talker. But talk is cheap, and I'm the first to admit it. It wouldn't be right to expose a problem without presenting possibilities to right the wrong. So here are some practical ideas on how godly men can actively support their sisters.

1. Speak up for them. This is the most obvious answer, and the easiest to do. When we men see women being treated unfairly, overlooked, or excluded from areas where they should have a voice, somebody needs to say something. Yes, men, it will likely put you in the line of fire. But consider that the women have already taken far more hits *just by being women* than you will take by standing up for them. You can handle the heat. Be respectful to your brethren, but tell it like it is. Change doesn't come unless someone with a voice confronts the problem.

2. Enable them on purpose. Entire books could be written on what this might look like, but the idea is that men need to go the extra mile to help women recover their voice and place. For a season, this might even look unbalanced in the other direction, like we are giving women more advantage. But the reason this season of enabling is necessary is that after many centuries of stifling and restricting women, we have essentially made the "weaker sex" even weaker—just like muscles atrophy when we don't use them.

Let's look at an example of what enabling might look like. When a church first opens leadership opportunities to women, there are still apt to be far more men who meet the qualifications for those roles than women, because the men are accustomed and prepared to lead, while the women have not been. If we're not careful, we'll take the passive approach in this situation and let it be an excuse for keeping males at the helm. But if we are going to take the extra step to enable our sisters, we could create opportunities for education and training specifically geared for the women, in order to *help* them qualify, to balance the scales of advantage—so that no matter who is best suited to lead at that time, at least the *opportunity* to qualify is more balanced. Again, this is just one possibility of many. But enabling our sisters means we will look for ways to help them erase their disadvantage, not just leave them to figure it out for themselves.

3. Honor them. I personally believe there is a spiritual significance to this, because again, it is the righting of a wrong. Whether intended or not, our restrictions and suppressions of women in the church (and generally treating them as inferiors in other ways) have dishonored them. There is something powerful and healing that takes place when a man publicly affirms and celebrates the gifts and qualities a woman brings to the table. But it's important to mention here that honoring our sisters must not become over-compensating or patronizing. Rather, it must become a genuine attitude, something that works into our lifestyle and our overall treatment of women.

4. Make room for them. It actually takes a personal humbling for men to do this, but if we are serious about being part of the solution, part of that process involves placing extra chairs at the table, and when necessary, stepping aside to let a woman have our seat. If a man is afforded an opportunity to lead in some capacity, for example, and there is a woman who is equally able and willing to do so, it is an honorable thing for that man to prefer his sister over himself. I think actions like these are an important part of the healing process, because it sends a clear message that we are no longer making the women contend for their place at the table, but instead offering it to them, welcoming them into that place.

5. Finally, we need to listen to them. At the very heart of this issue, deeper than theological views or authority structures or equal opportunity, is the simple fact that by distorting the Scriptures, we haven't just labeled the woman as subservient or inferior, *we have robbed her of her voice.* We have told her that she must be "silent," and when she does speak, her words do not carry the same weight as a man's words. For healing to take place, we men cannot just give the women a platform on which to speak; we also need to *hear what they are saying.* When we listen with both ears, we might begin to understand more of their plight, and why this issue is so important to so many of them. And when we take their input seriously, we will likely find some wisdom we have not found by keeping our own counsel—wisdom that might save us from pitfalls and snares that in times past we have fallen into.

In all these things, it's important to note that by taking a more active role in restoring our sisters, we men are doing much more than just making up for past mistakes. By doing these things with sincerity of heart, we are literally taking the shackles off of essentially 50 percent of the image of God. For so long, we have figuratively been operating with one hand tied behind our back. By untying the woman's hands, and by loosing her voice, we are freeing ourselves.

I understand and acknowledge that among those in the church who have held the long-standing traditional view of gender roles, many (if not most) of these are well-intentioned people trying to do God's will. So by saying these things, I'm not trying to villainize them. However, we need to recognize that it is just this well-intentioned sincerity that has over the years been a subtle tool in the enemy's hands. I personally believe that ever since the Garden of Eden, Satan has had a special vendetta against the female of our species, and one of his favorite tricks is to subvert truth with just enough deception to make us work against ourselves. Indeed, some of the most destructive acts in history have been performed by Christians fully convinced they were doing God's will. I realize this sounds a bit strong, but we need to see this for what it is. We need to see that, through the misuse of Scripture, the enemy pitted us against our sisters. He has used us to place our foot upon their necks when he has been unable to do so—all in the name of honoring the Word of God. In so doing, we have damaged and crippled ourselves.

Thankfully, this tide is turning, and more and more people are beginning to see that the plan of God for women was much greater than this, that He never intended for the woman to have a lesser place or a lesser voice. Slowly but surely, the feet are coming off of the necks. This is a wonderful thing.

Hopefully I have conveyed that ceasing from standing on our sisters' necks is only the first step of restoration. Our sisters also need us to extend our hands to them and lift them up—to lend them our strength as men until they have recovered enough strength to take flight in their own God-given strength.

Jeff McQuilkin is a minister in transition, a worship leader and house church pastor who served for years within institutional Christianity, and is now finding fresh expression outside the walls. He lives with his wife and 19-year-old son in Tulsa, Oklahoma. You can catch up with his current ramblings at his blog, "Losing My Religion."

13

Wikiklesia Volume 2 Taking Flight
Dancing As Well As Weeping
Thomas Hohstadt

We could easily blow this moment in history. After eons of patriarchal privilege, the debate over a woman's "place" has hopefully passed, but our "enlightened" solutions could make matters worse.

We point our finger at those "other guys" in past cultures that distorted gender issues so tragically, not realizing that every culture "has its bias, its particular prejudice," or, as Voltaire called it: "The lie commonly agreed upon." For example, "liberation," "fairness," "success," "equality," and "freedom" may inspire our gendered spokespersons, but they do little to confront more fundamental issues. Phrases like "realizing their potential" and "compared to men" may resonate our sympathies, but they do less to reflect more urgent issues.

Today's "enlightened" women, for example, yearn for the less male-dominated language of the Greeks with their "gods" and "goddesses." This is not so difficult to imagine, for our culture is more Greek than it is Judeo-Christian. We have long filtered the Gospel through formula, analysis, theory, and conjecture—a learning not only "skeptical," but super-skeptical. But the feminine spirit will find no consolation here. The emotions and feelings of the Greek "soul" were considered "ungodly," a "sign of weakness," and even a "source of evil."

Hebrew women knew a different knowing. Life was not a mere idea. Through their own raw experience, they grasped unspoken revelations suddenly and intuitively. Rather than the disembodied wisdom of the Greeks, they knew an **embodied** wisdom: heightened sensitivities to "felt meanings"—visceral feelings, heartfelt emotions, and ecstatic joys. These were **redeemed** passions, and they knew them as their source of strength—not as a sign of weakness.

Their prophetic wisdom did not provide the easy answers of today's "liberation," "fairness," "success," "equality," and "freedom." Instead, Hebrew women met God in the unresolved tensions—the fundamental contradictions—the enigmatic mysteries **between** men and women.

This strange, reciprocal relationship—this inspired interplay between differences and resemblances—proved the very language of God. Hosea explains that God speaks to us by placing side-by-side things that are supposedly the same, yet fundamentally different.[1] The resulting juxtaposition reveals a transparent and transcendent Otherness which we intuitively recognize as the "the Word made flesh"—the Incarnate Word.

---

1 In Hosea 12:10, the language of God is called *damah* (in the original Hebrew). Often translated as "parables" or "similitudes," a better translation would be "prophetic metaphor." Yet in our modern literary world, the word "metaphor" has lost much of its original power. Today, it is usually a mere literary device for "colorful language" or "figures of speech." The early Hebrew writers intended a "juxtaposition"–or profound tension–between things that cannot be compared. Further, they knew that through that tension, truth or meaning is often revealed that lies beyond the juxtaposition itself. Today, the theologian Tillich would say this *damah*, or profound juxtaposition, "points only out of the power to which it points." For further information, see Harris, Archer, and Waltke, *Theological Wordbook of the Old Testament, Volume I* (Chicago: Moody Press, 1980) pp. 191, 192.

This truth was grasped by later writers. Johann-Georg Hamann wrote, "Divine truth appears only through . . . contradictions."[2] And Søren Kierkegaard echoed, "All existential truth is paradoxical . . . (and) the language of revelation . . . (is) absolute paradox."[3]

Is the paradox of this gender gap comfortable? Of course not. Yet, Scripture confronts us with endless contradictions. Paul, for example, continually points to these painful absurdities: Joy is in your sufferings! Power is in your frailty! Life is in your dying! In all of his writings, in fact, Paul juxtaposes endless pairs of opposites: shame and honor, suffering and comfort, frustration and glory. . . .

Yet, today's gender arbiters stubbornly avoid this "language of God." Their "journey of freedom and reconciliation" flees this enigma and paradox of Scriptural truth. For their vision of the "female half of God's image" usually "takes flight" **away from** the male half of God's image.

Further, their "enlightened" escape does little to make up for the ongoing battle between "flesh" and "spirit." For example, there have always been three types of women: the "shrew," "the siren," and "daddy's little girl." (Men have their own problems.[4])

The "shrew" must aggressively demand her "rights" with men. She must win the battle with men—beat them at their own game! And the extremists among them have become "castrator-terrorists."

---

[2] Johann Georg Hamann, quoted in Louis Dupré, *Symbols of the Sacred* (Grand Rapids: Eerdmans, 2000) p. 58.

[3] Louis Dupré, *Symbols of the Sacred* (Grand Rapids: Eerdmans, 2000) p. 58.

[4] Male counterparts include "bullies, romantics and mama's little boys." The idea for these female/male categories came from an unpublished poem by Gene Marshal (written in 1967 for the Ecumenical Institute in Chicago.)

The "siren" wins her way by seducing men (whether in or out of bed). This temptress finds success by exploiting her relationships with men. And she intentionally dresses to empower her intentions.

"Daddy's little girl" sweetly submits while getting her own way. She is the "gentle manipulator." And, sometimes, the fear of a male-dominated "Otherness" sends her into the arms of "safer" female relationships.

Yes, of course, it's possible for God's beauty and power to flow through **redeemed** personalities, but women never fully rid themselves of these basic inclinations.

Even so, the "Lord of History" is giving women their moment of grace today. For we are returning to the power of an oral tradition where "Life happens at the level of events not of words"[5]—where life interprets "spiritual truths with spiritual language"[6]—and where life is "taught by the Spirit with language appropriate to the Spirit."[7] It's a major shift from logic to revelation, from mind to spirit, from proposition to paradox, and from the literate to the prophetic.

It is the ultimate incarnate dialogue, where Spirit takes on body, and body takes on Spirit. And this event is impossible without the intuitive emotions and feelings of embodied wisdom. The future belongs to those women who live this shift and embrace its wisdom.

---

5 Alfred Adler, http://www.insightquotes.com/a_author.htm

6 I Corinthians 2:13, AMP

7 Gordon D. Fee, *Paul, the Spirit, and the People of God* (Peabody, Massachusetts: Hendrickson Publishers, 1996) p. 80.

We must dare to imagine the ecstatic joy and feminine mystery beyond "religious" traditions. We must dare to re-image the quiet light and gentle heart of God's "mystic rose." Perhaps, we're not looking for "success" or "liberation." Perhaps, we're looking for those who will come into God's presence with dancing as well as weeping.[8]

Dr. Thomas Hohstadt is a symphony conductor, author, and senior lecturer at The University of Texas of the Permian Basin. A lifetime study of the language of music and the future of the arts has revealed more than ordinary answers to some of the pressing issues of our time. His books include Dying to Live *and* A Prophetic Compass for the Emerging Church. *His website is www.FutureChurch.net.*

---

[8] Jeremiah 31:4, 9; AMP

Wikiklesia Volume 2 Taking Flight
The Weakest Foot Forward
Angie and Todd Fadel

Rights are never ours to be grasped. We should hold our rights loosely, relinquishing them whenever necessary to extend the kingdom of God or to protect a weaker member of the Body of Christ. The overriding principle Paul gave in 1 Corinthians—equal rights for men and women, but surrendering personal rights whenever necessary—can be applied wherever we find ourselves in ministry. — David Hamilton

Society often seems to use shorthand to deal with, or short circuit, painful cultural struggles. For instance, one of the most detrimental and pervasive of these societal shorthands is the arbitrary assignment of positions of "power" and "weakness." "Power" is bestowed on the streamlined, direct approach to struggle, and "weakness" on the more complicated, considerate approach. In other words, those regarding the greater whole while attempting to find a solution (or respite from the pain) are perceived as the ones that "bog down the process." Like a parent who gives the "because I said so, that's why!" answer to an inquisitive child, the overwhelming struggle and subsequent exhaustion can lead to power plays at the expense of engagement. At any rate, when expedience is given precedence, stereotype trumps story. When this happens, the fabric of the soul is in jeopardy of unraveling.

Males, who have typically been given the position of "power," and females, who have typically been given "weakness," spend a good portion of their lives either developing their positions or resisting them.

Angie: The word "weakness" in this context raises my hackles. It works on one level, but on another level it just makes me angry at the typical "fairer sex" or "weaker sex" comments we're all familiar with.

Todd: Should we change it?

Angie: It's just that I want it to be clear that we're leading up to talking about weakness that's chosen, not imposed.

Todd: Agreed.

No one is immune to the influence of these societally-imposed positions. For instance, the harmful shortfalls of power could look like showing a lack of consideration to the degree of feeling entitled to an irresponsible behavior. On the other hand, weakness can turn into an over-consideration of others to the detriment of self, which is just as harmful. Resisting either position requires understanding the flaws and the positive attributes at the heart of these positions.

First, let's look at the flaws that power can have. Power demands unified thought and can consume reflective reasoning. It may have no interest in compromise or democratic decision-making, and its strength is commonly wielded through fear and intimidation. Power can be exploitative, simultaneously building up and tearing down, but it can also be transformative.

Angie: Power looks different when a man wields it, too.

Todd: How do you mean?

Angie: When I assert myself, a certain code seems to get set in motion. Men who are unwilling to share influence label me negatively and justify exclusion. I don't get listened to.

Todd: Can't you fight for your influence?

Angie: I can, but I find myself thinking, "Are we still here? I want to be 20 miles down the road from here." This same conversation, one that my sisters have been having all these years, keeps coming up and nothing seems to change. But, if power and influence is used to give others a voice, that's a completely different story.

Weakness carries a different set of flaws. Weak wills can be easily overwhelmed by reality, and weak minds can be corrupted. But weakness can also be flexible with difficult situations. It would rather support than exploit. In 2 Corinithians, the apostle Paul makes an interesting statement: that the Power of God is perfected in weakness. In other words, the secret to the revelation of God's character and strength lies in the attributes of weakness. Note that the quote states His Power is *perfected*, not just enhanced. From this standpoint, those who are acquainted with the position of weakness (whether by choice or not) should be listened to and revered as keepers and protectors of a Holy gift.

Todd: Does it make sense to say it that way?

Angie: Maybe, but so much of what is expected of me becomes an overwhelming swirl of activity and I get lost in it.

Todd: It's like when those commercials for mattresses ask, "Are you tired after a day of doing the housework, working at the office, and picking up the kids from soccer practice? You need a mattress. "And the women are like, no, I need to re-negotiate my partnership so I'm not taking on so much.

Angie: Or when people push me to blog or twitter—I don't have room in my life to do that, so I get overlooked, while those that can are listened to.

Todd: What can I do to help you not be overwhelmed?

Angie: Like most women, I have to deal with the expectation that I pour myself out for others, without any consideration for myself. I'm not used to verbalizing my needs.

Todd: Can't you just stop thinking that way?

Angie: Can't you just stop disengaging?

Todd: Ouch.

Angie: The difficulty with "just stopping" is that these expectations are reinforced everywhere, constantly. Especially in churches. This is not the type of weakness that is chosen, this is imposed.

As resistance to the flaws of these positions becomes clearly necessary, one tendency is to respond with a knee-jerk *tokenism*. Tokenism is an attempt to quickly rectify an unjust situation by appearing compassionate, but it can cloud any detrimental principles that created the situation in the first place. It is simply another unhelpful shortcut. This must sink in. To resist is to work toward replacing these flawed cultural uses of power and weakness, and to accept the mess that will ensue. We must work to replace *imposed weakness* with *chosen weakness* for the purpose of seeing God work through His people.

Some stories and practices

After one Sunday service, we were approached by a friend who, up until that day, had made the decision that he would not sing aloud in public. What helped him muster up the courage to risk singing in public again was when he heard Todd's singing voice, which is consistently flat and cracking. Todd's "passion over precision" showed our friend that the point of participating is to share his voice *just because it was his*, and that makes it *valuable.* The weakness of one helped free another.

Another friend recently gave us lyrics to a song she had written. She doesn't consider herself to be a songwriter, but she offered herself to us anyway in weakness, in vulnerability. Todd and I will make every effort to share her song with others whenever we can because we want to honor the risk she took in trusting us with it.

Notice how our friends offered themselves to us and our community in weakness expressed by their *play*. Singing and songwriting are forms of playing, aren't they? And it is becoming more and more apparent to us that play is a crucial, inclusive piece of our collective spiritual growth. When a child plays, she takes an idea and moves forward with it. When another child enters that environment, the first child has a choice: to accept the interaction of the additional person, or to reject them and continue on alone. Children learn early on that an accepting play environment works by relinquishing an amount of control, by an act of chosen weakness. So, in our community, we have deliberately put our playful selves "to work" by creating new games as an excuse to exercise our weakness together. Some of our games are musical, but the form/medium we choose is not the point—what is valuable is learning how to be weak.

The stories we draw from our people is the gold we're mining for: their unique perspective, their accounts of God's interaction with them, descriptions and anecdotes that define their motivations, aspirations, and limitations.

A word of caution

Inviting these inclusive environments carries with it a sobering reality. A community that chooses weakness must take steps to ensure that cynics, naysayers, and opportunists do not take advantage of the vulnerable. Healthy protection of authenticity and safeguards against abusiveness start out well-intentioned, but it is imperative that a new regime of reactionary facilitation does not take root. Communities must be vigilant to make clear the distinction between vulnerable acts and power plays.

Musical Caravanning

Everyone is familiar with the experience of being stuck behind a lousy caravanner. A successful caravan is when everyone arrives at the destination together. A group of us assemble every other week with our instruments to jam together. It is an open invitation and no one is turned away, no matter what skill level. Step by step, we walk through tuning, scales, rhythm, and chords. Many people arrive with no training whatsoever, but by the time we're done, we are all playing a chord (at least) in time. Some have shared that was the first time they had ever felt confident with music because they were allowed to learn at their own pace without fear of humiliation.

Ink Brethren

Another game we play uses collaborative improvisation. This requires a certain attraction to recklessness, while maintaining an environment where everyone is kept intact. Song titles are brainstormed by a group of four or more, a director loosely suggests a song framework (tempo, mood, instruments, storyline) based on a chosen title, and the record button is pressed. A "song" happens from that moment to when the stop button is pressed. During the "songs," the group learns how to support one another's musical ideas in real-time.

The Whirrship

This game is a multi-community, multi-media, non-musical (mostly) collaborative experiment in fostering the ideas of children. We listen to how a child looks at her world and we attempt to re-create it into a staged production with whatever recycled materials are readily available. People from 12 different churches worked together on our last performance piece, which integrated improvisational poetry, cardboard sculptures, collage costumes, projection art, and paper-cup percussion.

Storytelling

Our more "experienced" voices have stories that need to be captured and shared. This game helps develop the art of prompting and listening. A kiosk is set up at a local gathering spot for retirement-aged individuals and our younger people create the vibrant, accepting environment where storytelling runs wild. Those elder storytellers who want their stories captured for loved ones are given free DVD copies.

Matchbook

More a tool than a clearly defined game, the matchbook is simply a piece of paper folded to make 32 panels on each side. These can be made into 4 separate mini-books for different creativity prompts. What is significant about the matchbook is that it can be used for innumerable experiments. Most recently, we have used a matchbook to make mini puppet shows, sketchbooks, battleship games, and collections of poetry.

The point

As the weakest members are considered and followed, a broader view of the cultural landscape becomes visible. In fact, the invisible starts to appear more frequently, made incarnate through the love and consideration of others. Play and collaboration fosters and sets the stage for the discovery of God's characteristics that have been long discarded. And when these Divine characteristics are revealed through the weakness that is willingly walked into by a loving community, the trials of life do not prompt fearful response—they are counted as joy.

Angie and Todd Fadel would like to think of themselves as conductors who conduct conductors that conduct. For the last 11 years, they have devoted themselves to creativity in community, specifically stationed at the Bridge in Portland, OR. Their focus helps fresh ideas get fleshed out. Three albums of songs have been released by "Agents of Future," the collective of artists and musicians at The Bridge. Also, "Love Is Concrete" is "a network of artists / content-writers / think tankers and a hub for resources that engage and explore the imaginations of our communities and help draw out the stories of God's interaction with us—almost like an agency/army of worship freelancers looking for projects to stretch out with." Dig deeper at www.thebridgeportland.org, www.loveisconcrete.com, and bit.ly/allaboutAOF.

"Our deepest wishes are whispers of our authentic selves.
We must learn to respect them. We must learn to listen."
—Sarah Ban Breathnach

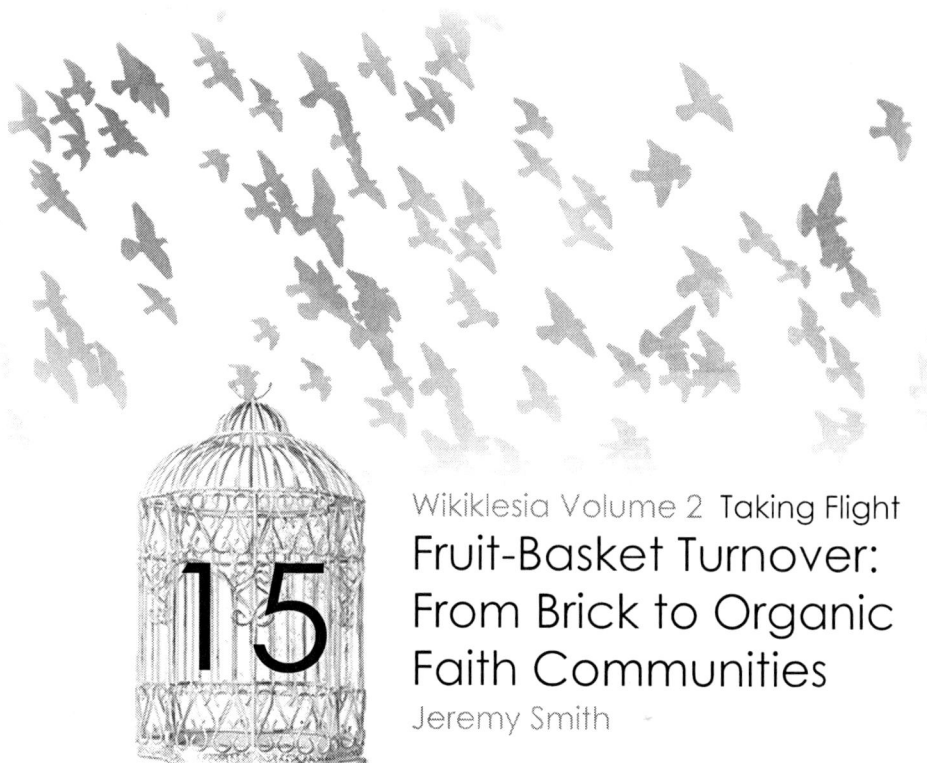

Wikiklesia Volume 2 Taking Flight
Fruit-Basket Turnover: From Brick to Organic Faith Communities
Jeremy Smith

> *In ecological terms, when one variable is changed, the entire system changes. How will women's voices change the emerging ecology of today's faith communities?*

In the Revelation to John, the City of God is outlined in exact detail: four walls with three gates each, equidistant corners, with the river of life flowing in a human-made canal in this city of straight lines and hard corners (Revelation 21-22).

Perhaps if the Revelation was instead to Joan, the city of God would not have a rigid conformity and hierarchical structure. Rather, an organically grown San Francisco-style city might be depicted of jumbled brickwork and stuccoes, containing lawlessness that nonetheless reflects the beauty of God. What might have changed in Christian theology if our vision of the City of God was more organic than created, more freewheeling than rigidly dictated?

We stand at the intersection of these two Cities: one built on rigid tradition, the next built on organic relationships in a wild untamed theological wilderness. The first has been ruled by men for at least nineteen centuries of the Christian tradition. The next nineteen centuries will be influenced heavily by women's voices.

Like a budding plant that splits the concrete, we stand at the cusp of an entirely new and beautiful form of the City of God. This City sheds tradition and breaks through the rigid conventions that refuse to yield. And it is perhaps women of faith who are the best positioned to understand, respond to, and build this emerging ecology.

At the outset, I offer one assertion I originally heard from ecological ethicist Marla Marcum: All theology is ecological, focused on relationships and relationality between parties, doctrines, and values. The rise of women's voices and participation in communities of faith is a challenge to every theological ecology simply because when one variable changes, it affects all others. While women, as we see in this Wikiklesia workgroup, have been influencing all along, the soil is ready for something new.

It is to our loss that traditional models of workplace and theological "diversity" place women's voices as "needed input" into the machine to make it more "relevant" and certainly more PR-friendly. This mechanistic model de-values women's roles and underestimates how women participate in faith communities.

The Internet age has changed the way businesses, organizations, communities, campaigns, and families form their relationships. Two of the leading internet theorists examining this shift are Clay Shirky, author of *Here Comes Everybody*, and Ori Brafman & Rod A. Beckstrom, authors of *The Starfish and the Spider*. While these are men, their writings offer insight into this brave new world that women are inheriting and will dominate.

In the days of Youtube, Flickr, Facebook, and blogs, people are used to creating things and sharing their creations. To this phenomenon, Clay Shirky writes about the virtuous circle between creating communities of value and valuing communal works. For instance:

> "...because enough people thought of using Wikipedia as a coordinating resource, it became one. And because it became one, more people learned to think of it as a coordinating resource." (Shirky 117)

This virtuous circle of creating has been a place where women have thrived for centuries. In Christine Pohl's book *Making Room* (1999), she writes about 4th-5th century women who were benefactors offering hospitality to the emerging movement of monasticism, which was itself a response to centralization of authority in Constantine's Christendom. Their hospitality helped begat centuries of monastic hospitality. Women helped birth monasticism—what will women help birth in this Internet Age?

Regardless of what niches or marks or leadership areas women influence, relationships will need to be made. Brafman and Beckstrom outline in *The Starfish and the Spider* the way that these relationships are nurtured or strained in the Internet Age. One factor is whether organizations centralize authority in fewer and fewer hands or decentralize it by dispersing it among the people. Be it reviewing eBay sellers, or editing Wikipedia, the tendency toward centralization or decentralization is a choice every relationship must make.

This is a salient point in theological circles and church structures as some seek to centralize and control the strained and stretched relationships of the Internet Age. I believe this is a factor behind the resurgence of Neo-Calvinism in recent years. For example, Seattle's thriving Mars Hill church embraces hyper-masculinity and discouragement of dissent.[1] But it is also evident in the centralized way churches respond to controversy and changing mission fields.

Centralizing authority is one direction churches can go, but decentralization is present as well. In an essay on my blog, I outlined "What the Church Can Learn From Wikipedia,"[2] and one lesson is to grab onto the "long tail" of small groups of 2-3 people.[3] These small groups often yield considerable influence in the life of the church and their small size yields transformative intimate relationships. This can revolutionize church budgets as they move resources away from broadcast mediums to intimate conversation. This can revolutionize professional ecclesiology as the power moves from the clergy (predominantly male) to the laity (predominantly female), bringing more women into ministry and gender parity in the ranks. What will women collaborate and co-create in the Internet Age?

In both of these theorists' ecologies of relationships, one factor springs forth: the locus of power is no longer in the tops of belfries, but in small groups who nurture and activate their passions. The Internet Age is coming to full bloom. Decentralized communication between diverse groups, from stay-at-home moms to house-church planters, allow for the entire church to be transformed one small group at a time.

---

1 http://www.nytimes.com/2009/01/11/magazine/11punk-t.html?_r=3&hp=&pagewanted=all
2 http://weare.hackingchristianity.net/series/wikipedia-church
3 http://blog.hackingchristianity.net/2008/05/what-church-can-learn-from-wikipedia_14.html

This is not all sunshine and puppy dogs—there is a painful growth process ahead of us. Distributed groups like we have been describing have overturned the fruit-baskets of the newspaper industry (Craigslist), the music industry (Napster), and the phone industry (Skype), none of which are really through the woods yet as of this writing, and all of their successors have been demonized in some way.

Likewise, the Church, in the short run, will experience painful changes with the emergence of reactionary theologies, schisms as small groups are empowered, and the crumbling of institutional unified social witness. But in the sunlight seen through the widening cracks in the stained glass ceiling, there is hope for those who persevere and take a chance to co-create this new City of God.

As faith communities are flattened and hierarchical authority is challenged in the Internet Age, women are best placed to lead faith communities to adapt to ever-changing conditions. As the traditional frameworks of religious and secular institutions are challenged and lose authority, a new type of authority and common language crafted by women may be the greatest hope for effective systems of relationships—that is, ecologies that value not only God and God's Creation, but the life-giving relationships between God's children as well.

@UMJeremy, a United Methodist minister, is convinced that nerds will inherit the earth. He blogs at "Hacking Christianity" (http://blog.hackingchristianity.net) about faith, technology, and Internet-Age group theory.

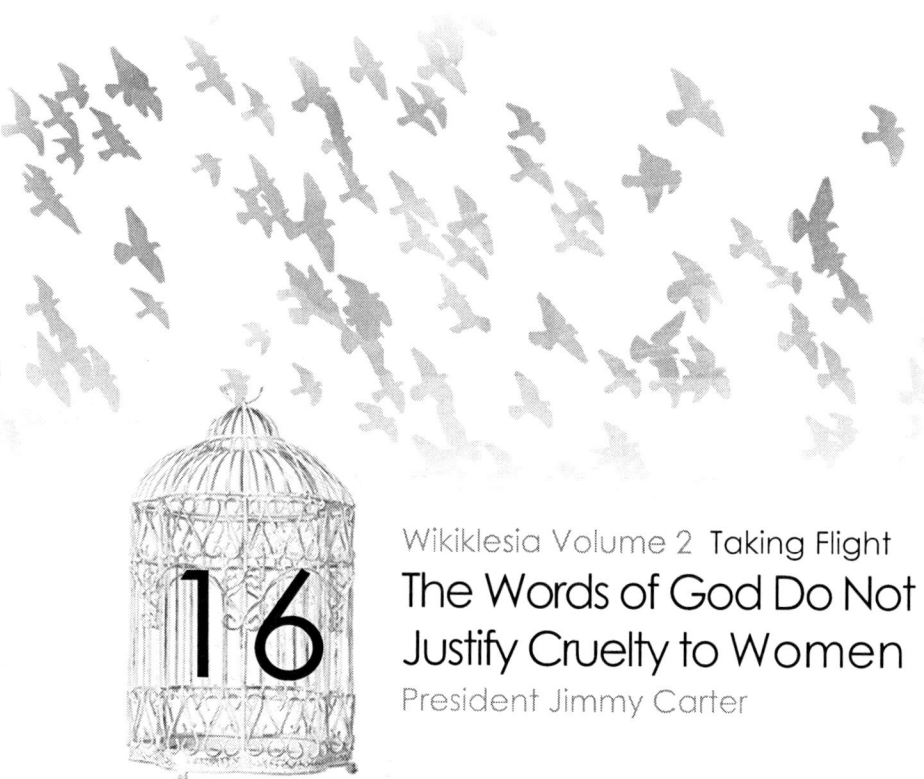

Wikiklesia Volume 2 Taking Flight
The Words of God Do Not Justify Cruelty to Women
President Jimmy Carter

> *"Everyone is entitled to all the rights and freedoms set forth in this Declaration, without distinction of any kind, such as race, colour, sex, language, religion, political or other opinion, national or social origin, property, birth or other status . . .."* (Article 2, Universal Declaration of Human Rights)

> *"There is neither Jew nor Greek, there is neither bond nor free, there is neither male nor female: for ye are all one in Christ Jesus."* (Galatians 3:28)

I have been a practicing Christian all my life and a deacon and Bible teacher for many years.[1] My faith is a source of strength and comfort to me, as religious beliefs are to hundreds of millions of people around the world. So my decision to sever my ties with the Southern Baptist Convention, after six decades, was painful and difficult. It was, however, an unavoidable decision when the convention's leaders, quoting a few carefully selected Bible verses and claiming that Eve was created second to Adam and was responsible for original sin, ordained

---

[1] Editorial by former U.S. President Jimmy Carter, published in the July 12, 2009, edition of *The Observer*.

that women must be "subservient" to their husbands and prohibited from serving as deacons, pastors or chaplains in the military service.

This view that women are somehow inferior to men is not restricted to one religion or belief. Women are prevented from playing a full and equal role in many faiths. Nor, tragically, does its influence stop at the walls of the church, mosque, synagogue or temple. This discrimination, unjustifiably attributed to a Higher Authority, has provided a reason or excuse for the deprivation of women's equal rights across the world for centuries.

At its most repugnant, the belief that women must be subjugated to the wishes of men excuses slavery, violence, forced prostitution, genital mutilation and national laws that omit rape as a crime. But it also costs many millions of girls and women control over their own bodies and lives, and continues to deny them fair access to education, health, employment and influence within their own communities.

The impact of these religious beliefs touches every aspect of our lives. They help explain why in many countries boys are educated before girls; why girls are told when and whom they must marry; and why many face enormous and unacceptable risks in pregnancy and childbirth because their basic health needs are not met.

In some Islamic nations, women are restricted in their movements, punished for permitting the exposure of an arm or ankle, deprived of education, prohibited from driving a car or competing with men for a job. If a woman is raped, she is often most severely punished as the guilty party in the crime.

The same discriminatory thinking lies behind the continuing gender gap in pay and why there are still so few women in office in the West. The root of this prejudice lies deep in our histories, but its impact is felt every day. It is not women and girls alone who suffer. It damages all of us. The evidence shows that investing in women and girls delivers major benefits for society. An educated woman has healthier children. She is more likely to send them to school. She earns more and invests what she earns in her family.

It is simply self-defeating for any community to discriminate against half its population. We need to challenge these self-serving and outdated attitudes and practices – as we are seeing in Iran where women are at the forefront of the battle for democracy and freedom.

I understand, however, why many political leaders can be reluctant about stepping into this minefield. Religion, and tradition, are powerful and sensitive areas to challenge. But my fellow Elders and I, who come from many faiths and backgrounds, no longer need to worry about winning votes or avoiding controversy – and we are deeply committed to challenging injustice wherever we see it.

The Elders have decided to draw particular attention to the responsibility of religious and traditional leaders in ensuring equality and human rights and have recently published a statement that declares: "The justification of discrimination against women and girls on grounds of religion or tradition, as if it were prescribed by a Higher Authority, is unacceptable."

We are calling on all leaders to challenge and change the harmful teachings and practices, no matter how ingrained, which justify discrimination against women. We ask, in particular, that leaders of all religions have the courage to acknowledge and emphasize the positive messages of dignity and equality that all the world's major faiths share.

The carefully selected verses found in the Holy Scriptures to justify the superiority of men owe more to time and place – and the determination of male leaders to hold onto their influence – than eternal truths. Similar biblical excerpts could be found to support the approval of slavery and the timid acquiescence to oppressive rulers.

I am also familiar with vivid descriptions in the same Scriptures in which women are revered as pre-eminent leaders. During the years of the early Christian church women served as deacons, priests, bishops, apostles, teachers and prophets. It wasn't until the fourth century that dominant Christian leaders, all men, twisted and distorted Holy Scriptures to perpetuate their ascendant positions within the religious hierarchy.

The truth is that male religious leaders have had – and still have – an option to interpret holy teachings either to exalt or subjugate women. They have, for their own selfish ends, overwhelmingly chosen the latter. Their continuing choice provides the foundation or justification for much of the pervasive persecution and abuse of women throughout the world. This is in clear violation not just of the Universal Declaration of Human Rights but also the teachings of Jesus Christ, the Apostle Paul, Moses and the prophets, Muhammad, and founders of other great religions – all of whom have called for proper and equitable treatment of all the children of God. It is time we had the courage to challenge these views.

Jimmy Carter was US president from 1977-81. The Elders are an independent group of eminent global leaders, brought together by Nelson Mandela, who offer their influence and experience to support peace building, help address major causes of human suffering and promote the shared interests of humanity.

> "Every generic religious text encourages believers to respect essential human dignity, yet some selected scriptures are interpreted to justify the derogation or inferiority of women and girls, our fellow human beings."

> "Most Bible scholars acknowledge that the Holy Scriptures were written when male dominance prevailed in every aspect of life. Men could have multiple sex partners (King Solomon had 300 wives and 700 concubines), but adulterous behavior by a woman could be punished by stoning to death - then, in the time of Christ and, in some societies, 2009 years later."

> "It is ironic that women are now welcomed into all major professions and other positions of authority, but are branded as inferior and deprived of the equal right to serve God in positions of religious leadership. The plight of abused women is made more acceptable by the mandated subservience of women by religious leaders."

Selected quotes from a speech by Jimmy Carter delivered by remote video from Atlanta, GA to the Parliament of the World's Religions, Melbourne, Australia, Dec. 3, 2009

The most beautiful things in the world are
not seen nor touched. They are felt with the heart.
--- Helen Keller

17

Wikiklesia Volume 2 Taking Flight
The Courageous Imagination:
A Call to Men
Jonathan Brink

If we look outside the front windows of neighborhood homes and see little boys exploring their glorious imagination through play, it is almost inevitable that at some point they will pick up two sticks and pretend to fight. Deep within the heart of a man is the desire to express his masculinity through aggression. The question then becomes whether we are fighting *with* someone or *for* someone?

What would it look like to live with a courageous imagination, one that would require men to step up to a fierce, sacrificial love for women? What would it look like for men to correct our destructive bent to rule over women? Can we begin to reshape the male imagination in a way that encourages the deep and immense honor that it is to lift women up for the sake of our own humanity.

It is impossible to ignore the history of oppression that is embedded within culture towards women. We speak and act from position, place, and power. We are the ones who have historically controlled the polity, the pulpit, and the home. And in that place we have subjugated women to a secondary role. Yet is it possible that in that subjugation, we have ignored half of our own voice?

If we are honest about our own humanity we can't ignore the history of the great divide that exists in our own hearts. Humanity, or Adam, originally created in the Image of God, included both the woman and the man. The female, pulled from our own rib, represents the critical "other" half to our own judgment. We cannot see the full image of God in our midst without this other half. Discovering the whole image of God then requires lifting up and listening to the female voice.

So what happened? How did this divide come to pass? The answer lies in the sacred narrative of creation.

"Your desire will be for your husband, and he will rule over you." Genesis 3:16

The women's natural bent became to seek her validation in the man. But he would be unable to handle this request, using it instead to "rule over" her. This divided the whole Image of God. The man lost part of himself by subjugating her—in other words, he oppressed himself by oppressing her.

Consequently, the woman defined and defended the one role she was empowered to play, that of being a mother. Yet this role came at the expense of the relationship between the man and the woman.

We men bear a large portion of the responsibility for that problem. In subjugating and oppressing women, in limiting them to certain exclusive roles, we propagate and support a culture that deeply affects our own marriages, families, and social structures.

The original mandate to humanity was to rule over creation, not over each other. The temptation to rule produces a terribly crippling burden that we are ill prepared to hold. Yet we hold onto it because it is culturally acceptable.

When we oppress women by cutting out their voices, their participation, and their calling to leadership, we have cut ourselves off from the whole picture of our humanity. We have oppressed ourselves. An entire half of God's image is missing from our midst.

The good news is that God is not standing idly by while we distort His image. Through the sacrificial love of Jesus, He leads men to discover the best move possible: relinquishing their control at the foot of the cross. The greatest act of restoration is found in sacrificing for the other, rather than ruling over the other. Jesus' example is profound—he had every right to take control and rule over us, yet he chose to take the road less traveled and found redemption in turning over that right.

There is something fierce about sacrificial love. The honor and dignity of fighting for someone speaks to our souls in ways that only the poets can capture. Shakespeare brilliantly captured this courageous imagination in King Henry V's speech to his men on St. Crispen's day:

"And say 'To-morrow is Saint Crispian.'
Then will he strip his sleeve and show his scars,
And say 'These wounds I had on Crispian's day.'
Old men forget; yet all shall be forgot,
But he'll remember, with advantages,
What feats he did that day."

Our St. Crispens Day comes when we take up the call to fight for the women in our midst. To fight for the voice of women is to fight for our own restoration. We cannot be whole without both the man and the woman represented fully in content, conversation, and decision. We cannot see the whole image of God in our midst without both parts of our own humanity.

To fight for someone reminds us of our dignity as human beings—it reminds us that we are part of a humanity that was once called very good.

The restoration Christ offers begins today

This is not something to think about. We must step up and completely change the way we live—by grace, invitation, and permission, rather than by shame, rejection, and fear. And by permission, I mean we must validate the permission that God has already given to women. Permission is not ours to give.

We must own our history as the male half of God's image, even if we didn't participate past oppression. We must seek forgiveness from the women around us, reminding them that it is our part to redeem the oppression we have created.

For those leading businesses, families, and churches, especially pastors, it means taking the risk and elevating women to leadership. It means restoring the other half of not only our own image, but also God's voice in our midst. This will be a sacrificial move for some. It might mean putting a job at risk. But when we fight for someone, it will become one of the most defining acts of our lives.

Each man must declare, "I will not oppress myself by ruling over women." A powerful scene near the end of the movie *Braveheart* portrays such commitment to freedom and service:

> *"Aye, fight and you may die. Run, and you'll live . . . at least a while. And dying in your beds, many years from now, would you be willin' to trade all the days, from this day to that, for one chance, just one chance, to come back here and tell our enemies that they may take our lives, but they'll never take—our freedom!"*

Our freedom will only come when we stop participating in the oppression of women. It is time to remove our shame. It is time to step into our calling as men and love fiercely and fight against the most oppressive of enemies: *the lie that lures us to oppress each other.* When we do this, we will rediscover the beautiful, magnificent whole image of God and Him in our humanity.

Jonathan Brink is Managing Director of Thrive Ministries, and a spiritual formation coach. He is deeply committed to helping people discover and participate in God's mission of restoration and reconciliation by engaging the Way of Jesus. Jonathan holds a BA in Bible from William Jessup University and an MA in Organizational Leadership from Gonzaga University. www.jonathanbrink.com

Does not wisdom call, and understanding lift up her voice?
On top of the heights beside the way,
Where the paths meet, she takes her stand:
Beside the gates, at the opening to the city,
At the entrance of the doors, she cries out...
Proverbs 8:1-3

For Wisdom is better than jewels, and all things which may
be desired are nothing in comparison with her.
Psalms 8:11

Wikiklesia Volume 2 Taking Flight
Quotes

Balance

Bill Gates recalls once being invited to speak in Saudi Arabia, finding himself facing a segregated audience. Four-fifths of the listeners were men, on the left. The remaining one-fifth were women, all covered in black cloaks and veils, on the right. A partition separated the two groups. Toward the end, in the question-and-answer session, a member of the audience noted that Saudi Arabia aimed to be one of the Top 10 countries in the world in technology by 2010 and asked if that was realistic. "Well, if you're not fully utilizing half the talent in the country," Gates said, "you're not going to get too close to the Top 10." The small group on the right erupted in wild cheering.

"Jesus gave no explicit teaching on the role of women in the church. In fact, he left no teaching at all concerning women as a class of people.... He treated every woman he met as a person in her own right." —*Grenz, Stanley, Women in the Church: A Biblical Theology of Women in Ministry.* InterVarsity, 1995, p.71

Weakness and Power

"Remember no one can make you feel inferior without your consent."
—*Eleanor Roosevelt*

"The most common way people give up their power is by thinking they don't have any." —*Alice Walker*

"It takes more courage to reveal insecurities than to hide them, more strength to relate to people than to dominate them, more 'manhood' to abide by thought-out principles rather than blind reflex. " —*Alex Karras*

"You are a weak man if you use your physical superiority to assault and brutalize women." —*Desmond Tutu.*

Beauty is in the heart

"There is in every true woman's heart, a spark of heavenly fire, which lies dormant in the broad daylight of prosperity, but which kindles up and beams and blazes in the dark hour of adversity."—*Washington Irving, The Sketch Book*

"Far away there in the sunshine are my highest aspirations. I may not reach them, but I can look up and see their beauty, believe in them, and try to follow where they lead." —*Louisa May Alcott*

"Our deepest wishes are whispers of our authentic selves. We must learn to respect them. We must learn to listen."—*Sarah Ban Breathnach*

"The most beautiful things in the world are not seen nor touched. They are felt with the heart."—*Helen Keller*

Learning

"A woman uses her intelligence to find reasons to support her intuition." —*G.K. Chesterton*

"You can learn new things at any time in your life if you're willing to be a beginner. If you actually learn to like being a beginner, the whole world opens up to you." —*Barbara Sher*

"The most damaging phrase in the language is: 'It's always been done that way.'" —*Rear Admiral Grace Hopper*

Equality

"The day will come when men will recognize woman as his peer, not only at the fireside, but in councils of the nation. Then, and not until then, will there be the perfect comradeship, the ideal union between the sexes that shall result in the highest development of the race."

"Cautious, careful people always casting about to preserve their reputation or social standards never can bring about reform. Those who are really in earnest are willing to be anything or nothing in the world's estimation, and publicly and privately, in season and out, avow their sympathies with despised ideas and their advocates, and bear the consequences."
—*Susan B. Anthony*

"[A] woman should have every honorable motive to exertion which is enjoyed by man, to the full extent of her capacities and endowments. The case is too plain for argument. Nature has given woman the same powers, and subjected her to the same earth, breathes the same air, subsists on the same food, physical, moral, mental and spiritual. She has, therefore, an equal right with man, in all efforts to obtain and maintain a perfect existence.

"When the true history of the antislavery cause shall be written, women will occupy a large space in its pages, for the cause of the slave has been peculiarly woman's cause. —*Frederick Douglass*

Innovation often originates outside existing organizations, in part because successful organizations acquire a commitment to the status quo and a resistance to ideas that might change it. —*Nathan Rosenberg*

"In the faces of men and women I see God." —*Walt Whitman*

Wisdom

"For wisdom is better than jewels, and all things which may be desired are nothing in comparison with her." —*Proverbs 8:11*

"Pure gold cannot be given in exchange for it, nor can silver be weighed as its price." —*Job 28:15*

"Coral and crystal are not to be mentioned; and the acquisition of wisdom is above that of pearls." —*Job 28:18*

Wikiklesia Volume 2 Taking Flight
The Challenges Facing Women and Girls are Clear
Appendix 1

The informal slogan of the Decade of Women became, "Women do two-thirds of the world's work, receive 10 percent of the world's income and own 1 percent of the means of production." — *Richard H. Robbins, Global Problems and the Culture of Capitalism*

"Women and girls around the world face great challenges. They bear an unjust burden and this must change for the benefit of all humanity. We must act with common purpose and speak with one voice to change global policies and global wills so that gender justice and an end to poverty can be achieved." —*Archbishop Desmond Tutu, Honorary US-Breakthrough Summit Co-Chair (2008)*

- Women are 70 percent of the poorest and most vulnerable people on earth. At least 80% of humanity lives on less than $10 a day.

- Women represent two-thirds of the world's illiterate people. In the least developed countries, nearly twice as many women over age 15 are illiterate compared to men.

- Women make up 7 out of 10 hungry people in the world.

The Challenges Facing Women and Girls   Appendix 1

- Women do about 66% of the world's work for less than 5% of its income.

- Women produce 75% to 90% of food crops in the world, and they own one percent of the world's farmland.

- Women are dying at a rate of 600,000 each year from preventable complications of pregnancy. The life time risk of maternal death in Asia is 1 in 120. In developed countries it is 1 in 7300.

- Two-thirds of children denied primary education are girls, and 75% of the world's 876 million illiterate adults are women. (Less than 1% of what the world spent every year on weapons was needed to put every child into school by the year 2000 and yet it didn't happen.)

- According to UNICEF, an estimated one million children, mostly girls, enter the sex trade each year and the U.N. estimates that 4 million women and girls are trafficked annually.

- One in three women suffers physical, sexual, or other abuse by men during her lifetime. In some places, the figure can be as high as 70%. (U.N. Commission on the Status of Women, 2000)

- Sixty million girls who should be alive are "missing" from various populations, mostly in Asia, as a result of sex-selective abortions, infanticide, or neglect.

- When half the population is oppressed, all of humanity suffers. When women benefit the whole community benefits.

What's so important about half of the world's population?

- *What do women contribute to corporate financial performance?* On average, Fortune 500 companies with more women on their boards of directors turned in better financial performances than those with fewer women.[1]

- *What happens when women are employed in the third world?* When women and girls earn income, they reinvest 90 percent of it into their families, as compared with only 30 to 40 percent for a man.[2]

- *What happens when girls receive an education?* A one-percentage-point (ppt) increase in female education raises the average level of GDP by 0.37 ppt and raises annual GDP growth rates by 0.2 ppt on average.[3] Despite steady progress, two-thirds of the 759 million adults lacking literacy skills today are women.[4]

What happens when women across the globe have little to no access to health resources?

Each year, half a million mothers lose their lives in the process of giving birth. Millions more suffer complications that produce lifelong disability.[5]

---

[1] Ernst & Young, "Groundbreakers: Using the Strength of Women to Rebuild the World Economy," 2009.

[2] Phil Borges, Women Empowered: Inspiring Change in the Emerging World, 2007.

[3] United Nations, "Investing in Women and Girls," 2008.

[4] UNESCO, "Education for all," 2010.

[5] USAID, "USAID Global Health: Improving Global Health Improves the World," October 2009.

Wikiklesia Volume 2 Taking Flight
Belief Systems on the Roles of Women: Theological Constructs
Appendix 2

Attitudes and beliefs about the roles and responsibilities of women in Christianity vary considerably today, as they have throughout the last two millennia—evolving along with or counter to the societies in which Christians have lived.

The Complementarian[1] view asserts that women should remain in a submissive role according to the literal teaching of Scripture (1 Corinthians 11:3, 1 Timothy 2:12-14). The complementarian view of marriage maintains gender-based roles and a husband-headship structure in marriage. A husband is considered to have the God-given responsibility to provide for, protect, and lead his family, while a wife is to collaborate with her husband, respect him, and serve as his helper in managing the household and nurturing the next generation. The Bible instructs husbands to lovingly lead their families and to love their wives as Christ loves the Church, and instructs wives to respect their husbands' leadership out of reverence for Christ.

According to complementarian apologists John Piper and Wayne Grudem, male authority and female submission are integral to the "deeper differences," the "underlying nature," and the "true meaning" of

---

[1] http://en.wikipedia.org/wiki/Complementarianism

manhood and womanhood. These authors further maintain that men have the inherent right and responsibility to lead, while women are meant to be in submission to male leadership in the church and family.

The Christian Egalitarian view[2] refers to the biblically-based belief that gender, in and of itself, neither privileges nor curtails a believer's gifting or calling to any ministry in the church or home. The Egalitarian interpretation of scriptures and spiritual convictions brings them to the conclusion that the manner and teaching of Jesus abolished discrimination against racial minorities, slaves, and women, in both the church and marriage. They believe that the Bible, properly interpreted, teaches the fundamental equality of believers of all racial and ethnic groups and all economic classes.

This view does not imply that women and men are identical or undifferentiated. Christian Egalitarianism affirms that God designed men and women to complement and benefit one another. They believe the exercise of spiritual authority, as biblically defined, is deemed as much a female believer's privilege and responsibility as it is for a male. In Christ there is no longer any distinction in spiritual privilege or status between Jew and Gentile, slave and free, male and female (Galatians 3:26-28). Husband and wife are equal heirs of God's gift of life (1 Peter 3:7). Every believer is an adopted child of God, a recipient of the Holy Spirit and co-heir with Christ (Rom. 8:15-17, Acts 2:17-18).

They consider overarching principles of the Bible to be that men and women are equally created in God's image, equally responsible for sin, equally redeemed by Christ and equally gifted by God's Spirit for service, and equally held responsible for using their God-given gifts. A

---

2 http://en.wikipedia.org/wiki/Christian_egalitarian

significant source of this trend of thought is the Christian notion that humankind was created in the living image of God *(Imago Dei)*.

Christian feminism[3] is an aspect of feminist theology which seeks to advance and understand the equality of men and women morally, socially, spiritually, and in leadership from a Christian perspective. Christian feminists believe that contributions by women in that direction are necessary for a complete understanding of Christianity. Christian feminists believe that God does not discriminate on the basis of biologically-determined characteristics such as sex and race. Their major issues include the ordination of women, male dominance in Christian marriage, recognition of equal spiritual and moral abilities, reproductive rights, and the search for a feminine or gender-transcendent divine. Christian feminists often draw on the teachings of other religions and ideologies in addition to biblical evidence.

The first wave of feminism in the nineteenth and early twentieth centuries included an increased interest in the place of women in religion. Women who were campaigning for their rights began to question their inferiority both within the church and in other spheres justified by church teachings.

---

[3] http://en.wikipedia.org/wiki/Christian_Feminism

Wikiklesia Project: Volume 1

Voices of the Virtual World:
Participative Technology and the Ecclesial Revolution

"Uttered like a prayer retrieved from the year 2030, spoken in a new tongue, a new form. Listen!" - Kevin Kelly, Co-Founder / Executive Editor WIRED Magazine.

VOICES explores the growing influence of technology on the global Christian church. We hear from more than forty influential voices, including technologists and theologians, entrepreneurs and pastors... from a progressive Episcopalian techno-monk to a leading Mennonite professor... from a tech-savvy mobile missionary to a corporate anthropologist whom Worth Magazine calls "one of Wall Street's 25 Smartest Players." Voices is a far reaching exploration of spiritual journey within a culture of increasingly immersive technology.

ALL proceeds donated to the Not For Sale Campaign, dedicated to ending human slavery in our time.

http://wikiklesia.wikidot.com/about-volume-one

Samizdat Creative Services provides hybrid publishing, professional editing, and creative consulting to authors and organizations who transcend the bounds of traditional publishing houses.

"Samizdat" is the secret writing and distribution of banned literature in the former Soviet Union. It is an underground press–literally "self-publishing house", but with a subversive twist. If the KGB nabbed you, you'd be sent to Siberia faster than you could say "Molotov cocktail."

For more information, **visit our website at samizdatcreative.com**, send an email to **caleb@samizdatcreative.com**, or call 720-984-2810.

"Like" us on Facebook at **www.facebook.com/samizdatcreative**
Follow us on Twitter at **samizdatcreativ**

Buy our books at our website, Amazon, your local bookstore, or download an e-book at **scribd.com/samizdatcreative.**

Now Available from Samizdat Creative

*   *   *

Reflections of Generosity, a new book by Sgt. Ron Kelsey, is about one Soldier's struggle to find restoration and peace beyond the grief and tragedy of war. Through powerful essays and artwork, Sgt. Kelsey shares his story to encourage Soldiers and their families preparing for another deployment to face the coming sacrifices with courage and hope.

The artists featured in the book are all part of a traveling exhibition dedicated in honor of US military communities.

*   *   *

Can there be any hope left when everything seems to be crashing around us?

David McDonald thinks so. He turns us to a vivid and radical vision that God gave one of his craziest prophets, Ezekiel, in order answer the cry of his people–a cry we echo today–"Our hope has perished, and we are cut off."

www.samizdatcreative.com/store

LaVergne, TN USA
13 August 2010
193208LV00005B/9/P